VECTOR GRAPHICS 2024 GUIDE FOR BEGINNERS

MECKANZIE GUDAWIN

Copyright © 2023 Meckanzie Gudawin

All rights reserved.

INTRODUCTION

In the burgeoning age of digital design, vector graphics have emerged as the cornerstone of crisp visuals and scalable art. As we usher in the year 2024, the world of graphic design witnesses rapid evolution, with new tools and techniques reshaping the creative landscape. The "Vector Graphics 2024 Guide for Beginners" is your compass to navigate this vibrant terrain, offering a foundational understanding of vector imagery's precision, versatility, and enduring appeal.

Welcome to the threshold of creativity, where your journey into vector graphics begins. Whether you are an aspiring designer, a student, an entrepreneur looking to DIY your brand visuals, or simply a curious mind with a penchant for digital art, this guide is tailored to set you on a path of discovery and mastery.

As you step into the realm of vectors, let's first understand what they are and why they are becoming increasingly essential in the world of digital design. Vector graphics are composed of paths, defined by a start and endpoint, along with other points, curves, and angles. These paths are formulated through mathematical equations, which means they can be scaled up or down to any size without losing quality. This scalability makes vectors an invaluable asset for everything from tiny mobile icons to expansive billboard advertisements.

Chapter 1 of this guide, 'Getting Started and Overview', is designed to ease you into the world of vector graphics. You'll learn about the different software options available, how to set up your workspace, and the key terms and concepts in vector design. This chapter sets the stage for your creative journey, ensuring you have all the necessary tools at your disposal.

Chapter 2 delves deeper into the nuances of vector graphics, distinguishing them from their counterpart—raster graphics. Here, you will gain insights into the strengths and limitations of vectors, learn when to use them, and understand the importance of format selection in your work. You will also explore the intriguing process of converting between vector and raster formats, a vital skill in a designer's toolkit.

As we move to Chapter 3, 'Basic Tools', your hands-on experience begins. This chapter introduces you to the selection tools that are the bread and butter of vector design. Mastering these will allow you to manipulate and refine your artwork with precision.

In Chapter 4, we explore 'Primitive Shapes', the building blocks of all vector illustrations. From the humble line to complex shapes, you'll learn to create and manipulate basic forms, laying the groundwork for more intricate designs. Exercises at the end of the chapter will provide a practical application of the skills you've learned.

'Z-Ordering', discussed in Chapter 5, introduces a crucial concept in creating depth and hierarchy in your designs. This chapter not only explains what z-ordering is but also guides you through the intricacies of layering objects to achieve the desired visual effect.

Boolean operations, the focus of Chapter 6, are where your designs begin to take on a sophisticated form. These operations allow for the combination, subtraction, and intersection of shapes, providing endless possibilities for creativity.

Transformation techniques, covered in Chapter 7, are transformative, quite literally. You'll learn about translating, scaling, and rotating objects, as well as more nuanced transformations like reflection, alignment, and distribution—skills that will enable you to manipulate and position elements in your design with ease.

Chapter 8 is all about 'Working with Text'—a critical aspect of vector design. From the basics of choosing fonts and styling text to the more complex tasks of converting text to paths and placing text on curves, this chapter equips you with the know-how to incorporate text into your graphics effectively.

Lastly, Chapter 9 encourages you to move 'Beyond the Basics'. It's where you'll be introduced to advanced techniques such as masking, adding effects, and using the pen tool to create custom shapes and bezier curves—a technique that adds sophistication to your designs.

As we embark on this educational odyssey through the Vector Graphics 2024 Guide for Beginners, keep in mind that the journey is as rewarding as the destination. With each chapter, you'll be encouraged to experiment and play, because the essence of learning design is not just in understanding the tools and techniques but also in seeing the world through a designer's lens—recognizing the interplay of shapes, lines, and textures that make up our visual world.

This introduction aims not just to outline the contents but to also illuminate the path ahead, highlighting the value and excitement that comes with acquiring a new skill set. The field of vector graphics is a dynamic one, brimming with potential for those who are ready to explore and exploit its vast possibilities. So, let's turn the page to Chapter 1 and take the first step into a world where creativity knows no bounds, and your imagination is the only limit.

The intricate dance of shapes and colors on a digital canvas is a symphony composed by vector graphics—a symphony that you are about to conduct. The "Vector Graphics 2024 Guide for Beginners" is not just a manual; it is a portal into a world where mathematics meets art, where precision is at play with imagination, and where the potential for creation is limited only by the confines of your vision.

In a time when digital presence is tantamount to visibility, the power of well-crafted design becomes pivotal. Vector graphics are at the heart of this digital renaissance, offering crisp lines, perfect curves, and a scalability that raster images can only dream of. With vectors, a logo can be as immense as a building or as minute as a favicon, without ever losing the sharpness that defines it. This ability to scale infinitely is what makes vectors the preferred choice for branding, illustration, and interface design.

This book is carefully structured to take you on a step-by-step journey. Each chapter unfolds new concepts, tools, and techniques, building on the previous one to create a comprehensive learning experience. Starting with the foundational elements, you will progress through more complex ideas, until you are equipped with a robust toolkit of skills.

The creative world you are entering is both vast and intricate, encompassing a range of applications. A grasp of vector graphics opens doors to careers in graphic design, product packaging, book illustrations, user interface design, and even animation. In this digital era, vector design skills are highly sought after, not only for their aesthetic appeal but for their functionality across various media and platforms.

Understanding the fundamental differences between vector and raster graphics will be your first milestone. This knowledge will empower you to make informed decisions about the format that best suits your project's needs. Converting between the two formats is a skill that will prove invaluable, as it allows for flexibility and adaptability in your workflow.

Chapter 3's focus on 'Basic Tools' is the equivalent of learning the notes before playing a piece of music. By familiarizing yourself with selection tools, you'll begin to understand how to manipulate and control the vector elements you create. Mastery of these tools is akin to a painter knowing their brushes—it is the start of your fluency in the language of vector design.

Moving on to 'Primitive Shapes' in Chapter 4, you will learn how even the most elaborate designs begin with simple shapes. This understanding is pivotal. Like the alphabet to language, primitive shapes are the building blocks of all vector art. Through exercises, you will practice crafting and combining these shapes, developing an intuition for design and composition.

With the knowledge of 'Z-Ordering' in Chapter 5, you'll see how arranging these shapes can create the illusion of depth, enhance the storytelling of your piece, and bring clarity to complex compositions. This knowledge will elevate your artwork from flat images to pieces with dimension and hierarchy.

Chapter 6's exploration of 'Boolean Operations' could be likened to learning the grammar of design. Boolean operations are the syntactic rules that allow for the manipulation and interaction of shapes. These operations—uniting, subtracting, intersecting—serve as the framework within which your design elements relate to each other.

'Transformations', discussed in Chapter 7, are where your design comes to life. Much like a choreographer positions and moves dancers to create a performance, you will learn to translate, scale, and rotate your elements to tell a visual story. This chapter not only teaches you the mechanics of these transformations but also the artistry.

In Chapter 8, when you work with text, you'll understand that typography is not just about making words readable; it's about giving them voice, emotion, and resonance. Whether you're designing a logo or setting the type for a book cover, the ability to manipulate text is a powerful tool in your arsenal.

The final chapter before you leap beyond the basics invites you to complex techniques that demand a steady hand and a creative mind. Masking, effects, and the pen tool will be your instruments to add finesse and detail to your designs. Here, you will learn to master the pen tool—a skill that stands at the core of vector work—allowing you to create custom shapes and intricate paths.

The journey through this book is designed to be engaging, with exercises that not only reinforce the concepts you learn but also challenge you to apply them in creative ways. Every chapter is an invitation to explore, and each page turns to reveal more of the rich tapestry that is vector graphics.

As you traverse the landscape of this guide, remember that each chapter is not an island, but part of a larger continent. The skills you learn will interlace, the knowledge you gain will build upon itself, and the experience you acquire will be cumulative. Your progress will be a testament to the integration of these skills, culminating in a comprehensive understanding of the vector graphics that are so integral to modern visual communication.

CONTENTS

Chapter 1: Getting Started and Overview 1

Chapter 2: Introduction to Vector Graphics 4

Chapter 3: Essential Tools for Vector Design 22

Chapter 4: Mastering Basic Shapes 24

Chapter 5: Layering with Z-Order 41

Chapter 6: The Power of Boolean Operations 47

Chapter 7: Art of Transformation 60

Chapter 8: Typography in Vector Graphics 76

Chapter 9: Advanced Vector Techniques 91

Conclusion 109

CHAPTER 1: GETTING STARTED AND OVERVIEW

HOW DO VECTOR GRAPHICS WORK?

A series of instructions or mathematical assertions that arrange lines and shapes in a two-dimensional or three-dimensional space are used to produce vector graphics, which are computer pictures.

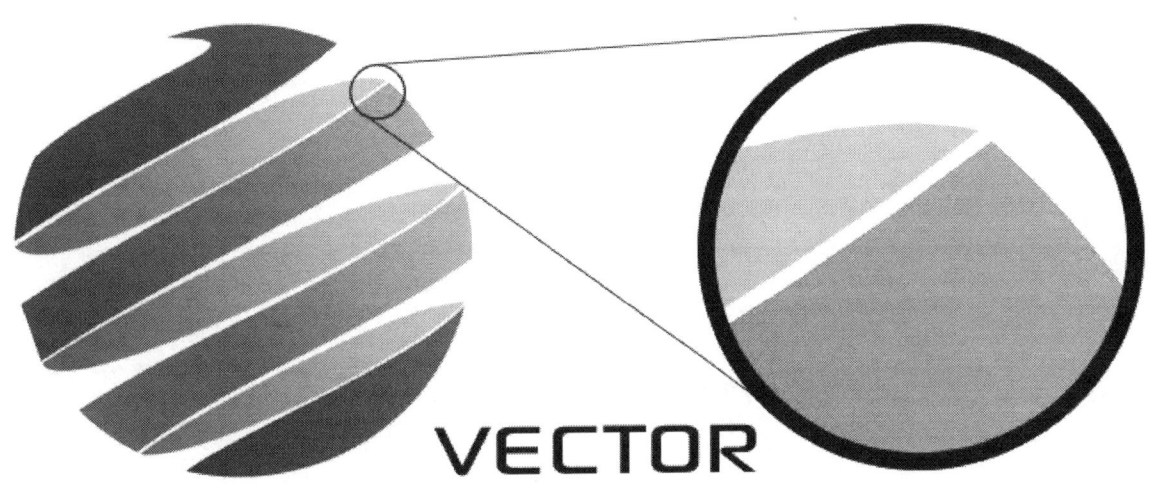

A graphic designer creates and saves their work as a series of vector statements in vector graphics. A set of points that need to be joined is described in a vector graphic file.

Sometimes these files are referred to as geometric files. Vector image files are typically used to store images made using programs like Adobe Illustrator and Corel's CorelDRAW.

Vector images that have been streamlined resemble connect-the-dots pictures.

What purposes serve vector graphics?

Vector graphics are used by designers, illustrators, and graphic artists for a number of purposes, including the following:

Scalability. Projects requiring scalable images, including scaled type and text, benefit from using vector formats. For instance, corporate and brand logos are shown in various sizes; they appear in the corner of a mobile application or on a billboard along the side of the road. A logo made using vector graphics may be resized without sacrificing quality or growing a file size.

After losing popularity to raster graphics in the 1980s, vector graphics made a comeback because to their capacity to scale. In the 1960s and 1970s, computer screens first employed vector graphics. The Scalable Vector Graphics open source language, which has both vector and raster components, is a result of work done by the World Wide Web Consortium on the Vector Markup Language.

Website and app development. Because online applications and the visuals they contain must function across a variety of screen sizes and device kinds, vector graphics are helpful in application and web development. For instance, the mobile app Amazon WorkLink allows employees to view fully interactive representations of business data on their devices.

Animation. Vector files are frequently used to create animated pictures because they produce visuals that are smoother and cleaner.

CAD, or computer-aided design. Because of its scalability and simplicity of updating the mathematical formulae, vector files are often used in CAD tools for manufacturing, engineering, and design.

Raster versus vector

Raster graphics images, commonly known as bitmaps, map bits directly to a display area. Raster graphics are less scalable than vector graphics because they consist of a fixed number of pixels. When the raster picture is sufficiently expanded, the edges start to seem ragged and it starts to look pixelated, or when the pixels are visible. Raster graphics cannot be enlarged without deteriorating the image.

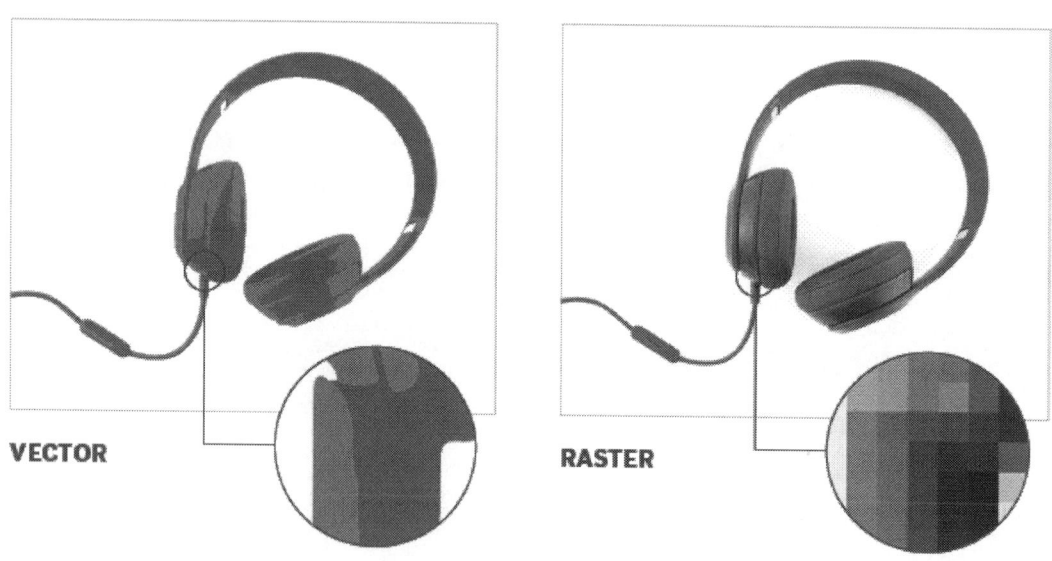

Additionally, there is a 1:1 correspondence between each pixel and the amount of memory that raster graphics need on a computer. In contrast to vector pictures, which merely store the sequence of points that need to be connected by lines, curves, etc., raster images need computers to keep information for every pixel. Since they are smaller than raster files, vector files are often smaller. For this reason, vector picture files are simpler to edit than raster image files.

With the appropriate tools, vector and raster pictures may be combined. Software that enables users to convert between different picture formats includes Adobe Illustrator and Adobe Photoshop.

Because each pixel may be a distinct color, raster files are very effective at displaying color depth. Additionally, there are more pixels than vectors that can have distinct colors. Raster file formats are therefore suitable for modifying digital photos.

Vector and raster components can be found in several file types; PDF and SVG files are two examples.

Vector graphics: pros and drawbacks

It is crucial to weigh the advantages and disadvantages of utilizing vector files.

advantages/disadvantages of raster and vector data models	raster	vector
precision in graphics	X	✓
traditional cartography	X	✓
data volume	X	✓
topology	X	✓
computation	✓	X
update	✓	X
continuous space	✓	X
integration	✓	X
discontinuous	X	✓

Advantages

Scalability. As was already established, this is vector graphics' major benefit. The reason vector graphics look precise and tidy at any scale is that they are generated from mathematical vector connections, or interactions between points that produce lines and curves.

Little file size. Because they only record a small number of points and the mathematical connections between them, vector graphics often have tiny file sizes. When opposed to storing images, code requires less memory to convey such relationships.

simple to modify. Users may quickly alter vector relationships to switch out colors or alter line forms, for example, making vector files simple to modify. This is helpful in an iterative process that calls for extensive editing, such as graphic design.

load quickly. Vector files may be easily loaded and transferred to a variety of hardware and software because of their modest file sizes.

simple to replicate. Additionally, it is simple to duplicate vector images and transfer certain elements from one graphic to another.

Precision. Since vector graphics may be scaled up or down, they offer a precise appearance and feel.

Disadvantages

less details. Complex image handling is limited for vector files. For instance, color shading and mixing are needed for images, which vector files are unable to deliver as effectively as raster files.

Time and skill constraints. The creation of vector files might take more time and expertise.

limited support for browsers. Web browsers support raster images more extensively than vector graphics.

Inconsistency. The characteristics of vector pictures might differ from one program to the next, among other things depending on how well-integrated the rendering and creation apps are.

Types of vector files

There are several commonly used vector file types. They include the following:

.ai -- Adobe Illustrator File

.cdr -- CorelDRAW Image File

.dxf -- Drawing Exchange Format File

.eps -- Encapsulated PostScript File

.svg -- Scalable Vector Graphics File

.wmf -- Windows Metafile

Vector and raster file features compared

	VECTOR	RASTER
Made up of	Lines, curves, shapes	Pixels
Convertibility	Can be converted to a raster file	More difficult to convert to vector file; special tools can help
Scalability	Scalable	Quality degrades when scaled
File format examples	.ai, .cdr, .eps, .svg	.gif, .jpg, .png, .tiff

For various tasks, many file formats are utilized. For instance, print media and computer graphics frequently employ AI files. Both raster and vector files may be stored in EPS files. They frequently include a modest design component that may be included in a bigger design. They may thus transmit logos, which are frequently incorporated into larger designs, thanks to this.

OVERVIEW

Chapter 2 Overview

In this second chapter of "Vector Graphics 2023 Guide for Beginners," we delve into the heart of vector graphics, aiming to provide you with a comprehensive understanding of this essential digital design tool. This chapter sets the stage for your journey into the world of vector graphics by answering fundamental questions and addressing your concerns.

We begin by identifying the target audience of this book, ensuring that both novices and experienced designers will find valuable insights within its pages. We also discuss the prerequisites you'll need to follow this guide effectively, emphasizing that you don't need Adobe Illustrator or costly software to get started.

To lay a strong foundation for your vector graphics knowledge, we break down the concept of vector graphics, explaining what it means and how it differs from raster graphics. You'll gain insight into various vector graphics formats and their advantages. This chapter also covers raster graphics formats, highlighting the distinctions between the two.

An essential part of your vector graphics journey is understanding how to convert between vector and raster formats. We explore the process of converting from vector to raster and from raster to vector, ensuring you have a grasp of these key transformation techniques.

By the end of this chapter, you'll be equipped with the fundamental knowledge required to embark on your vector graphics adventure, regardless of your prior experience or the software at your disposal.

Chapter 3 Overview

In "Vector Graphics 2023 Guide for Beginners," Chapter 3, titled "Basic Tools," takes readers on a fundamental journey through the essential tools that form the backbone of vector graphic design. This chapter serves as a solid steppingstone for newcomers to the world of digital design, offering a comprehensive understanding of the core tools at their disposal.

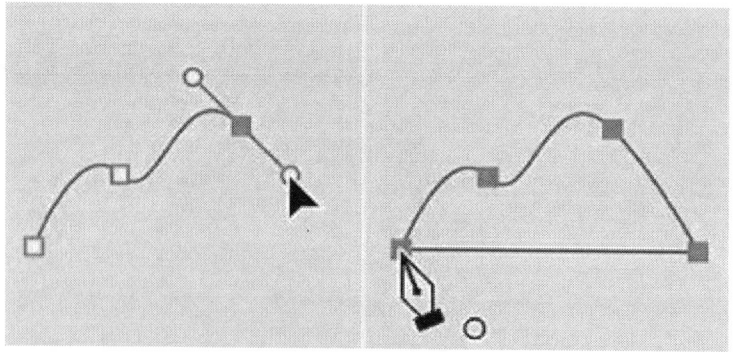

The chapter begins with "Getting Started & Basic Tools," ensuring readers are well-equipped to embark on their design journey. It covers the basic principles of vector graphics, setting a strong foundation. Subsequently, "Basics" delves into the heart of vector graphics, explaining the concept of vectors, shapes, and how they differ from traditional raster images.

The chapter also explores "Selection Tools," which are indispensable for manipulating and refining your designs. Here, readers learn how to select and modify elements with precision, an essential skill for every vector graphic artist.

With this chapter's guidance, beginners will gain the confidence and knowledge needed to navigate vector graphics and move forward in their digital design journey.

Chapter 4 Overview

This chapter is your gateway to the world of vector design. We begin by dissecting the building blocks of vector graphics, starting with lines. You'll learn how to create and manipulate lines, mastering the essentials of stroke and dash options. Moving on, we explore other basic shapes, such as rectangles, ellipses, and polygons, providing insights into transforming and aligning them. An important tip on working with filled shapes underscores the importance of efficient design practices.

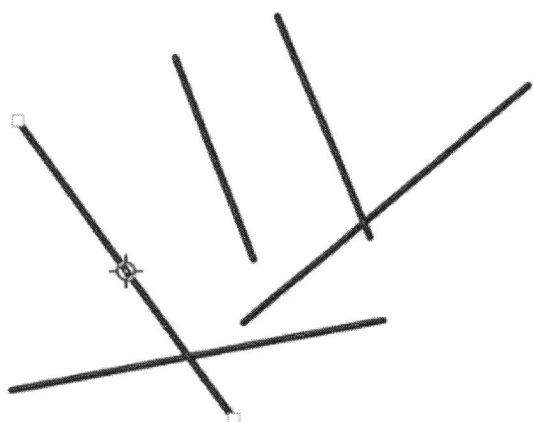

We'll guide you through the creation of primitive shapes, teaching you to construct various elements that form the foundation of vector graphics. Fills and strokes are explored in depth, along with the concept of gradients, allowing you to add depth and dimension to your designs. To reinforce your learning, we provide a hands-on exercise where you'll create a folder icon, integrating all the skills learned in this chapter. Finally, two stimulating exercises, "Freestyling'" and "Create a Simple Tennis Racket," await, offering a chance to apply your newfound knowledge and creativity. By the end of this chapter, you'll be well-equipped to craft visually captivating vector designs.

Chapter 5 Overview

In this chapter, titled "Z-Ordering," we delve into the fascinating world of manipulating the arrangement of objects in vector graphics. Z-ordering plays a pivotal role in design, determining the visual hierarchy and layering of elements within your artwork. This chapter equips beginners with a comprehensive understanding of Z-ordering and its application in digital design.

We start by unraveling the concept of "What's z-ordering?" to provide a solid foundation for the readers. Exploring how different elements stack up in vector graphics, we discuss the significance of this arrangement and its impact on the final composition.

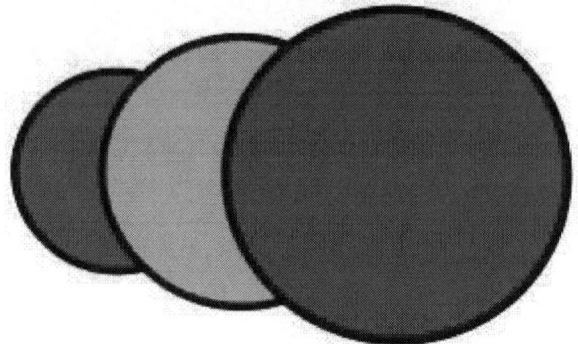

Next, we guide you through the process of "Modifying the z-order of objects." This section explores practical techniques and tools used to reposition elements within your vector design, ensuring your creative vision comes to life.

To further enhance your skills, we offer "Practical z-ordering tips." Here, you'll discover expert advice and best practices to efficiently manage and manipulate the z-order of objects in your design projects.

As a hands-on learning experience, this chapter concludes with "Z-ordering: Chapter exercises." These exercises challenge you to apply your newfound knowledge, reinforcing your proficiency in managing object arrangement. By the end of this chapter, you'll be equipped to create visually compelling vector graphics with precision and creativity.

Chapter 6 Overview

In Chapter 6 of "Vector Graphics 2023 Guide for Beginners," we delve into the fascinating world of Boolean operations within vector graphics. This pivotal chapter sheds light on the fundamental concept of Boolean operations, a vital skill for any aspiring digital designer.

The journey begins with a comprehensive explanation of what Boolean operations are and why they are essential in the world of vector graphics. We demystify these operations, making them approachable even for beginners.

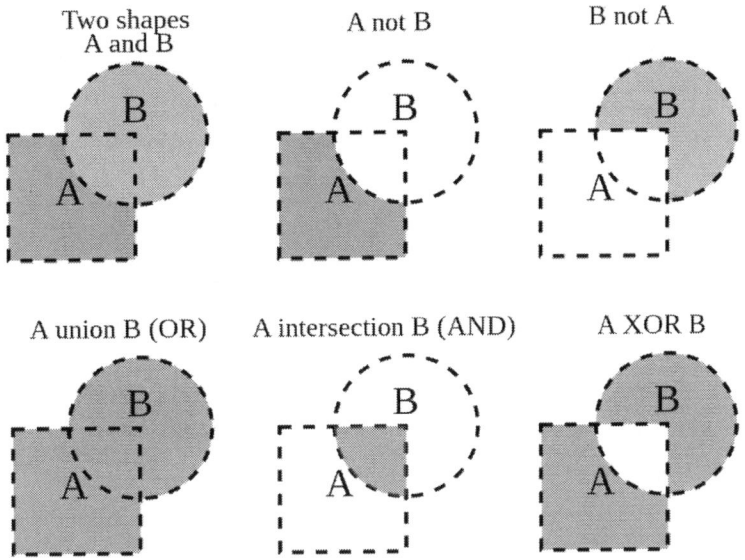

With the basics firmly in place, we guide you through the process of performing Boolean operations step by step. You'll grasp how to unite, subtract, intersect, and exclude shapes to create intricate designs.

Furthermore, the chapter demonstrates the practical applications of Boolean operations with real-world examples. Learn how to craft a crescent moon, simulate waves, conjure up a cloud, and craft an outline lightbulb icon. These hands-on exercises provide invaluable insights into applying Boolean operations creatively.

To reinforce your understanding, Chapter 6 also includes a set of engaging exercises, allowing you to test and hone your skills in Boolean operations. By the end of this chapter, you'll be well-equipped to leverage this essential technique in your vector graphic designs.

Chapter 7 Overview

We start by unraveling the intricacies of Translation, explaining how to smoothly move and reposition objects within your vector canvas. We then transition into the concept of Scaling, revealing the secrets to resizing elements while maintaining their proportions.

Rotation is the next subject of exploration, demystifying how to pivot, spin, and turn objects to create dynamic effects in your designs. Understanding how to alter the Center of Rotation is vital for precision and creativity.

The quirky-sounding Reflection AKA flippetyflips section teaches you the art of creating mirrored images, opening up new avenues for symmetrical designs. Alignment and Distribution techniques ensure that your design elements are neatly arranged and perfectly spaced.

We wrap up the chapter with Transformations: Chapter Exercises, featuring two practical exercises - Exercise 1: Practice and Exercise 2: Create a sword - to help you apply the knowledge you've gained in a hands-on manner. These exercises are designed to reinforce the principles covered in this chapter, making it easier for you to incorporate transformations into your vector graphic creations with confidence and skill.

Chapter 8 Overview

In "Vector Graphics 2023 Guide for Beginners," Chapter 8 delves into the captivating realm of text manipulation within the vector graphics landscape. This chapter equips readers with essential skills to infuse their designs with powerful typography, transforming text into a dynamic visual element. We explore the core aspects of text handling, including:

The text tool: Discover how to add, format, and customize text, opening the doors to endless creative possibilities.

Converting text to path: Uncover the secrets of converting text into editable vector shapes, granting you full control over each letter.

Neat trick 1: Applying a gradient fill to text: Learn how to make your text stand out by applying stunning gradient fills, adding depth and dimension to your design.

Neat trick 2: Playing around with a single letter: Take your text manipulation skills to the next level by dissecting and transforming individual letters.

Placing text on paths: Harness the power of text manipulation by placing it among various paths, from simple curves to complex shapes.

Using text as a mask: Explore the art of using text to create captivating, masked effects, providing a glimpse into advanced design techniques.

Each section is supplemented with practical exercises to reinforce your newfound knowledge and unleash your creativity. By the end of Chapter 8, you'll be well-versed in the art of working with text in vector graphics, ready to elevate your digital designs to the next level.

Chapter 9 Overview

In Chapter 9 of "Vector Graphics 2023 Guide for Beginners," we dive deeper into the world of vector graphics, taking you beyond the fundamental concepts and techniques you've learned so far. This chapter is a crucial steppingstone for those seeking to elevate their digital design skills.

Masking: We begin by exploring masking, a powerful tool that allows you to create intricate, visually stunning effects by selectively revealing or hiding portions of your designs. You'll learn how to harness the full potential of masking to add depth and dimension to your artwork.

Effects: This section delves into a wide range of effects that can transform your vector graphics. From shadows and gradients to glows and reflections, you'll discover how to enhance your designs and make them truly stand out.

Pen Tool, Anchor Points, and Bezier Curves: We thoroughly examine the versatile Pen Tool, providing in-depth insights into anchor points and Bezier curves. You'll master creating smooth curves and precise shapes, a fundamental skill for vector graphic artists.

Straight Lines & Curves: Understand the subtleties of drawing both straight lines and curves with the Pen Tool, giving you the control to craft intricate designs.

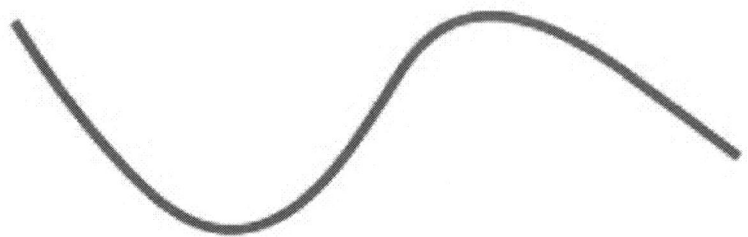

Anchor Point Types: Learn about the various types of anchor points and when to use them, enabling you to make your vector graphics more efficient and visually appealing.

Multi Selecting Anchor Points: Discover the art of selecting and manipulating multiple anchor points simultaneously, streamlining your design workflow.

Adding Anchor Points to an Existing Shape / Convert to Path: We demystify the process of adding anchor points to existing shapes and converting them to paths, empowering you to refine and customize your artwork.

Closed Paths vs. Open Paths: Understand the distinction between closed and open paths and how to use them effectively in your designs.

Practicing with the Pen Tool: To cement your knowledge, we provide hands-on exercises and practical tips to help you become proficient with the Pen Tool, ensuring you're ready to create vector graphics with confidence. This chapter equips you with the essential skills and knowledge to take your vector graphic design journey to the next level.

Chapter 2: Introduction to Vector Graphics

Who is this book for?

This book contains no animal products (except my heart and soul) and as such is suitable for vegans. I've been told that my soul definitely contains gluten and may also contain nuts, so consider yourselves warned.

If you've never done any work with vector graphics before, this is the book for you. You'll take your first baby steps by creating simple shapes like circles and rectangles and you'll finish this book with the skills required to create simple icons and logos. Along the way, I'll share tips and tricks that will take your abilities to the next level and give you exercises that will let you test your newfound skills in actual projects.

Prerequisites

Prior knowledge or experience in vector graphics is neither assumed nor required. Most common terms will be defined early on and reiterated throughout the book, so you'll never feel lost.

But I can't afford Adobe Illustrator

No problem. Most of the skills you'll learn from this book are transferrable to any vector graphics software. Teaching you the particulars of any specific application is not the point of this book. Showing you how to *think* about vector graphics is the actual point.

Of course, to be able to put your skills to the test and complete the exercises, you'll need some kind of vector graphics software but it really doesn't have to be Illustrator CC. It definitely can be Illustrator CC but here are some alternatives

- **Inkscape** (https://inkscape.org/): Yuck. Don't hate me, OSS fans. I've tried using it, but the whole thing is so convoluted and graceless I had to inject adrenaline straight into my heart just to stay alive and then I had to inject myself a second time to gather the courage to draw a circle. But, hey — it's free!
- **Gravit Designer** (https://www.designer.io/): Now this is more like it. The interface is clean and modern and it has power in spades. The basic program is also free, although you can subscribe to their PRO plan for (at the time of writing) $49/year. For the purposes of this book, the free version is going to be just fine.

- **Affinity Designer** (https://affinity.serif.com/designer/): Affinity Designer is not free but it's very affordable (55 euros at the time of writing) and while it's not as powerful as Adobe Illustrator, I'd say that it's pretty close.

If you don't already own a vector graphics software, just install Gravit Designer. It's free, it's fast, it's pretty and it's fully-featured. I'll be using it as a reference for the rest of this book, with occasional detours into Adobe Illustrator and Affinity Designer when needed.

Vector graphics? What are you talking about?

You're probably familiar with *graphics*, the visual representation of objects, ideas, and data on various mediums, such as paper, canvas or computer displays. For our purposes, we'll mainly be referring to images displayed on screens.

Computer graphic formats can either be vector- or raster-based. There's a world of difference between them, since raster-based graphics are *resolution-dependent*, while vector-based graphics are *resolution-independent*. If you've ever zoomed into a photo in a photo editor, you must have noticed that, as you kept zooming into it, the image would start to deteriorate until you were left with a jumble of colored squares. This happens because in raster-based graphics, such as a photo, the image is comprised of little squares called *pixels*. Think of pixels as the tiny tiles of a mosaic; when you look at a mosaic from far away, you cannot make out the individual tiles. It's only when you get really close that you can tell that what you've been looking at has been lots of intricately-placed tiles.

In vector-based graphics, the image is not described by pixels. Instead, the image is described by mathematical concepts and the relationships between them.

Too abstract? OK then, let me give you a concrete example: let's describe a standard lollipop in mathematical concepts and relationships. A lollipop is a spherical hard candy on a stick. The candy can be represented by a perfect circle, while the stick can be represented by a really elongated rectangle in a vertical orientation

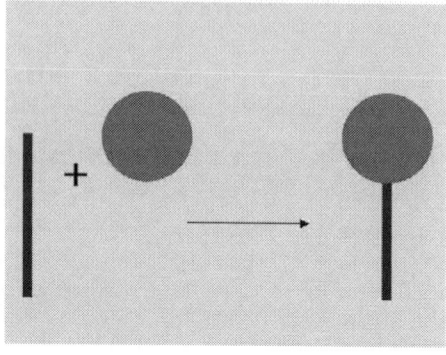

In the example above, we defined a rectangle and a circle and subsequently moved the circle over the rectangle and placed them in such a way as for the shapes to be centered on the x-axis, with the circle closer to the top end of the rectangle. As we'll discuss later, these shapes have more attributes than their purely dimensional ones, like fill color, stroke width, etc.

As you might imagine, unlike an image described by rectangles of a particular size in a particular configuration, this kind of description does *not* pixelate upon closer inspection. This is what we mean when we say that a vector graphic is resolution-independent. You can zoom into it all you want but the software knows that it should be rendering a scene defined by rules (not pixels) and updates the image accordingly.

Naturally, there are ways to convert between vector and raster formats and (in a more limited capacity) vice-versa. Before we explore how to do that, let's take a look at the most common raster and vector graphics formats.

Vector graphics formats

.ai: AI (Adobe Illustrator) is a proprietary format that can only be created by Adobe Illustrator. Software like Affinity Designer and Gravit Designer can import .ai files but they cannot create them. Due to the dominance of Adobe in the design industry, .ai files are pretty much the standard to be shared between designers or sent to clients.

.eps: EPS (Encapsulated PostScript) is a vector format that can be opened in most vector graphics software. EPS files contain a low-resolution raster version of the vector graphic it represents for easy preview.

.svg: SVG (Scalable Vector Graphics) is an open standard and it's a widely-supported format that can be exported from and imported into pretty much any vector graphics program.

.pdf: You may be surprised to hear, just as I was, that PDF (Portable Document Format) is a vector format. It would actually be more accurate to say that PDF *can be* a vector format but not all contents of a PDF file are guaranteed to be vectors. Indeed, if you embed a .PNG image into a PDF file, the PNG image doesn't magically turn from raster to vector. However, exporting a vector creation from inside Illustrator to PDF will retain the vectorness (vectorcity? vectorage?) of the image.

Raster graphics formats

.jpeg: JPEG (Joint Photographic Experts Group) is a format that's used for lossy compression of graphics, and especially photos. *Lossy* means that, after compression, the graphic that has been compressed has lost some of the original information it contained. That information has been lost forever and not even Stephen Hawking's ghost can pluck it out of the black hole it has fallen into. Which is to say, you cannot uncompress the graphic to retrieve the information that has been lost. **Exporting your vector designs to JPEG is not recommended because the format does not support transparency**.

.png: PNG (Portable Network Graphics) is a lossless raster format that supports transparency. *In your face*, JPEG! PNG files are perfect for storing the kind of graphics we will be creating in this book, like simple line graphics, flat illustrations and text-based designs.

More raster formats, like **.tiff** (Tagged Image File Format) and **.bmp** (Bitmap), exist and you may be asked to provide assets in these file formats too but we'll mainly be using the **.png** format in this book.

Converting between vector and raster formats

Converting from vector to raster

By their nature, vector graphics cannot be displayed in as many contexts as their raster counterparts. Vector formats contain *instructions* on how to draw something, while raster formats contain the image as a configuration of small rectangles. In addition to that, some vector formats are proprietary and operating systems do not have a native way of displaying them. This means that if you want someone to see a preview of a design you're preparing for them, it's better if you send them a raster version of the graphic instead of an .afdesign file (from Affinity Designer), an .ai file (from Adobe Illustrator) or a .gvdesign (from Gravit Designer) file.

To create a raster version of a vector graphic, you don't use the **Save** functionality in your graphics software. Instead, you use the **Export** function. Usually, you find this functionality in **File > Export**. From there, you can select the format you wish to export your design in.

If you're exporting a JPEG version, you'll be asked to select a quality level. The lower the quality level you select is, the smaller the file size of the image will be. If you select a quality level between 70% and 100%, your image is going to look fine after export. Going lower than 70% usually creates undesirable artifacts on the image, so try to stay within the aforementioned range.

If you're exporting a PNG version, you'll also be asked to select a compression level. "But hang on a minute," I hear you say. "I thought you said that the PNG format is lossless. Why is it asking me to select a compression level, if the end result is going to be the same anyway?"

In the case of PNG, the compression level corresponds to a higher level of encoding being applied to the image. This means that a PNG file that has had high compression applied to it will take longer to be decoded and displayed than a PNG file that has had lower compression applied to it. So unlike what happens with JPEG files, with PNG files what ends up happening is not a tradeoff in image quality — *it's a tradeoff in image loading time*. Smaller files take longer to be decoded and displayed than bigger files.

Converting from raster to vector

Taking a raster image and converting it to a vector one is a rather intricate procedure. While there's a clear path from a vector graphic to a raster one ("take what's in this window, create a pixel-based version, don't fuck it up") , converting a raster image into vectors means that the software that will be doing the conversion has to be able to trace the outlines of the objects in the image, which may be pretty simple for simple shapes but becomes incredibly processor-intensive for complicated images such as photos. I've been waiting for Gravit Designer to auto-trace a photo for me since the mid-nineties (ok, for the past five minutes) and it's still chugging away.

To convert an image into vectors, you need to first import the image into your vector graphics software. In Gravit Designer, you have to choose **Modify > Path > Vectorize** Image and wait. Like, *wait. A lot*. In Adobe Illustrator, you choose **Object > Image Trace > Make** and wait. Illustrator tends to be much faster than Gravit Designer at this sort of thing. Affinity Designer does not support this kind of functionality yet, so you'll need to use a third-party tool like Vector Magic (https://vectormagic.com/) to trace your images or use Inkscape's image trace tool to trace the image, export it to SVG and then load it into Affinity Designer.

Raster to vector is not something we'll be mentioning again in this book, but I wanted to mention that the functionality exists so that you know it's there should you need it in the future.

The five basic skills (*AKA The Good Stuff*)

Chapter 3: Essential Tools for Vector Design

If you still haven't downloaded a vector graphics program, now would be a good time to do so. To get the most out of this book, you should follow along with what I'm doing and then complete the exercises at the end of each chapter.

Do not think of the exercises as homework. Creating graphics in Gravit Designer, Adobe Illustrator or Affinity Designer is very similar to playing with legos, but for adults.

I'll be using Gravit Designer for the rest of this book, and there's a very good reason for that: it is, without a doubt, the least powerful of the three. If you learn how to create decent vector graphics within the limitations of Gravit Designer, gaining access to Illustrator's and Affinity Designer's more powerful features

(more boolean operations, object blending, spine replacement, Illustrator's inimitable Shape Builder tool, etc) later on will feel like you've been endowed with superpowers beyond your wildest imagination. Moreover, less powerful also means less complicated, at least in this case.

Basics

The first thing you should do when you open your software is to select one of the templates offered to you or create your own project from scratch. Usually, this involves selecting the dimensions of your project/canvas. Adobe Illustrator, Affinity Designer and Gravit Designer all offer a variety of print and device templates to help you get started.

We want to create a canvas of relatively small size, since a lower resolution means faster processing times when we're creating our designs. Either go for a square canvas of **768px by 768px** a landscape canvas of **1024px by 768px**

Gravit Designer lets you select your desired resolution with a pop-up dialog that opens up as soon as you start the software and log in. Enter the dimensions I gave you (make sure that you select **px**— pixels — as your units) and click **Create!**

You should see a blank canvas.

Selection tools

We'll be discussing most of the available tools in the rest of the book, but there are two that you should be familiar with right off the bat. These tools exist in all vector graphics programs and, while they may be named differently, they do very similar things.

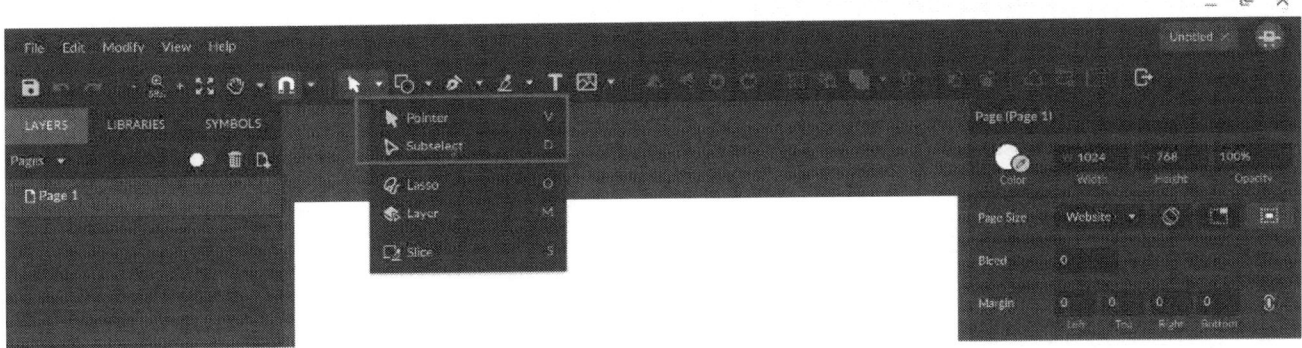

The first one of these tools is the **Selection** tool. The Selection tool looks like a cursor and it lets you select, move, rotate and resize objects. Clicking on an object with the Selection tool selects the object and lets you move it around by dragging & dropping it where you want. The rest of the operations facilitated by the selection tool will be described in detail later.

The second one is the **Subselect** tool (also known as the **Direct Selection** tool in Adobe Illustrator) which lets you select an object from a group of objects and also manipulate anchor points. A similar tool in Affinity Designer is called the **Node** tool. Anchor points/nodes are points on paths that let you modify the shape of the paths themselves, either by moving the points, changing the point type, altering the curvature of the path between the points or by manipulating the handles of the anchor point. See the 'Beyond the Basics' chapter for a more thorough discussion of anchor points and the closely related **pen tool.**

Finally, I'd be remiss not to mention the **Zoom** tool, which looks like a magnifying glass. You zoom in by pressing the '+' icon on its right and zoom out by pressing the '-' icon on the left. The Zoom tool is quite helpful for adding details and lining up shapes, among other things.

Chapter 4: Mastering Basic Shapes

Shapes. All of us know what shapes are: a circle is a shape. A square is a shape. Even a simple straight line is (arguably) a shape. Google agrees that the definition of a shape is "a geometric figure such as a square, triangle, or rectangle".

Creating shapes in a vector graphic program couldn't be easier. Most programs will provide you with a selection of shapes to choose from and all you have to do is pick the one you want to draw and then click and drag on the canvas to create a shape of the desired size. The number of available shapes varies depending on the software you use (Affinity Designer has a staggering amount of shapes available for you to use by default, including stuff like speech bubbles).

Shapes are underrated. Beginners in particular tend to scoff at them. What use could a circle and a rectangle be to them? What they fail understand is that

- Simple shapes will form the basis for most of their work in vector graphics
- Shapes can be customized to an impressive degree by simply changing some of their attributes
- Combining shapes and boolean operations (more on these in the relevant chapter) can create beautiful, intricate designs

Let's begin our examination of shapes by taking a look at the most common ones you will encounter.

Line

I know straight lines probably don't sound very exciting and maybe they are not, but we'll be examining them anyway. There's a very good reason for that and it's not because I hate you: examining such a simple construct will let us take a first look at the various attributes of **paths** and **strokes**, without having to worry about other aspects of the shape.

To start with, open your favorite vector graphics software and draw a line. To draw a line in Gravit Designer, you go to your toolbar and select 'Line' from the Shapes dropdown menu. Here's how it looks, with the selection you must make highlighted in red

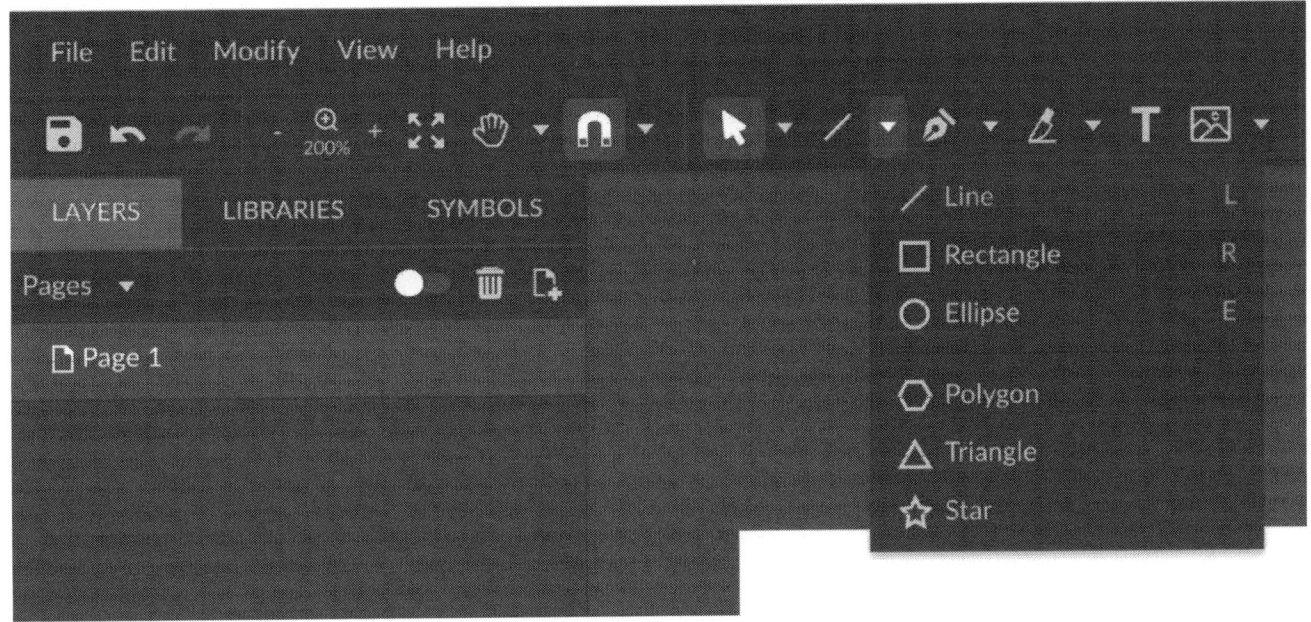

After you've selected 'Line', click somewhere on the canvas and, holding down the mouse key, drag your pointer to where you want the line to end. Once you're there, release the kraken. Sorry, I meant the mouse key. You should now have a straight line on your screen.

Like in many other programs, this is not the only way to create a line. Another way would be to use the pen tool, the fountain pen-looking icon next to the Shapes dropdown. More on the pen tool later.

Now that we have a test line down, let's take a look at its attributes.

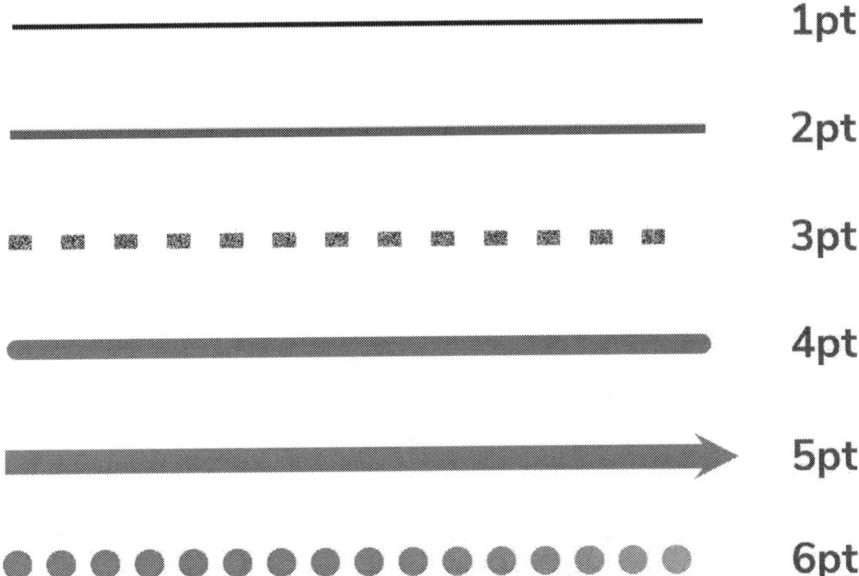

To start with, let's call these lines by their proper names: strokes. A stroke is a line that follows a path, be it a straight or a curved path. The difference between a stroke and a path is that the path is the mathematical, abstract representation of a line, while a stroke is the actual line that you draw on that path. To put it in the simplest terms, when you grab a piece of paper and a pencil to make a sketch, what you imagine that you'll put down to paper is the path, while the actual thing you draw is the stroke. Thankfully, in the case of computers, what they calculate is what they display on their screen. with no room for interpretation or trembling hands.

In the image above, you can see six strokes, with an increasing stroke width as you move down the list. As the stroke width increases, so does the width of the stroke. This sentence alone is probably enough to earn me a nomination for the 2020 Captain Obvious Awards. The 1pt stroke is black (stroke color) and has square ends, also known as caps (the terminal part on each side of the stroke).

Moving down the list, the 2pt stroke is purple and, again, has square caps.

Things get more interesting in the 3pt stroke, as there are a couple of new things going on: the stroke is **dashed** and it has been treated with a noise effect. Vector graphics programs let you create dashed paths by specifying a dash width (how long each dash will be) and a gap size (how big the gap between the dashed will be) for each stroke.

The 4pt stroke is blue and it has rounded caps/ends. I'm mainly including it so you can understand the difference between square caps and round caps.

The 5pt stroke is gray and it has an arrow at its end cap. That arrow is part of a collection of objects you can add to the start and/or the end of a stroke in Gravit Designer (and all other vector graphics programs).

The 6pt stroke is, again, very interesting. You may have noticed that its color is not uniform — instead, it gradually changes from a pinkish/purplish hue into an orange color. This is called a **gradient** and you can apply it to strokes and fills (more on fills later). Another thing you may have noticed is that the stroke consists of dots. This is actually a dashed path with the dash width set to 0
(zero), which is what most vector graphics programs use to generate a dotted stroke. You'll have to remember this one.

To recap, here's a list of the main attributes of a stroke:

1. Stroke width (numerical value, the biggest the wider the stroke is)
2. Stroke color (numerical value(s), uniform or gradient)
3. Type of stroke caps (square or rounded, with object added at the caps or not)

You're probably wondering how you can change all of these attributes. To do that, you need to go to the stroke settings panel. In Gravit Designer, once you've selected a stroke you'll find the stroke settings on the right side of the screen by default.

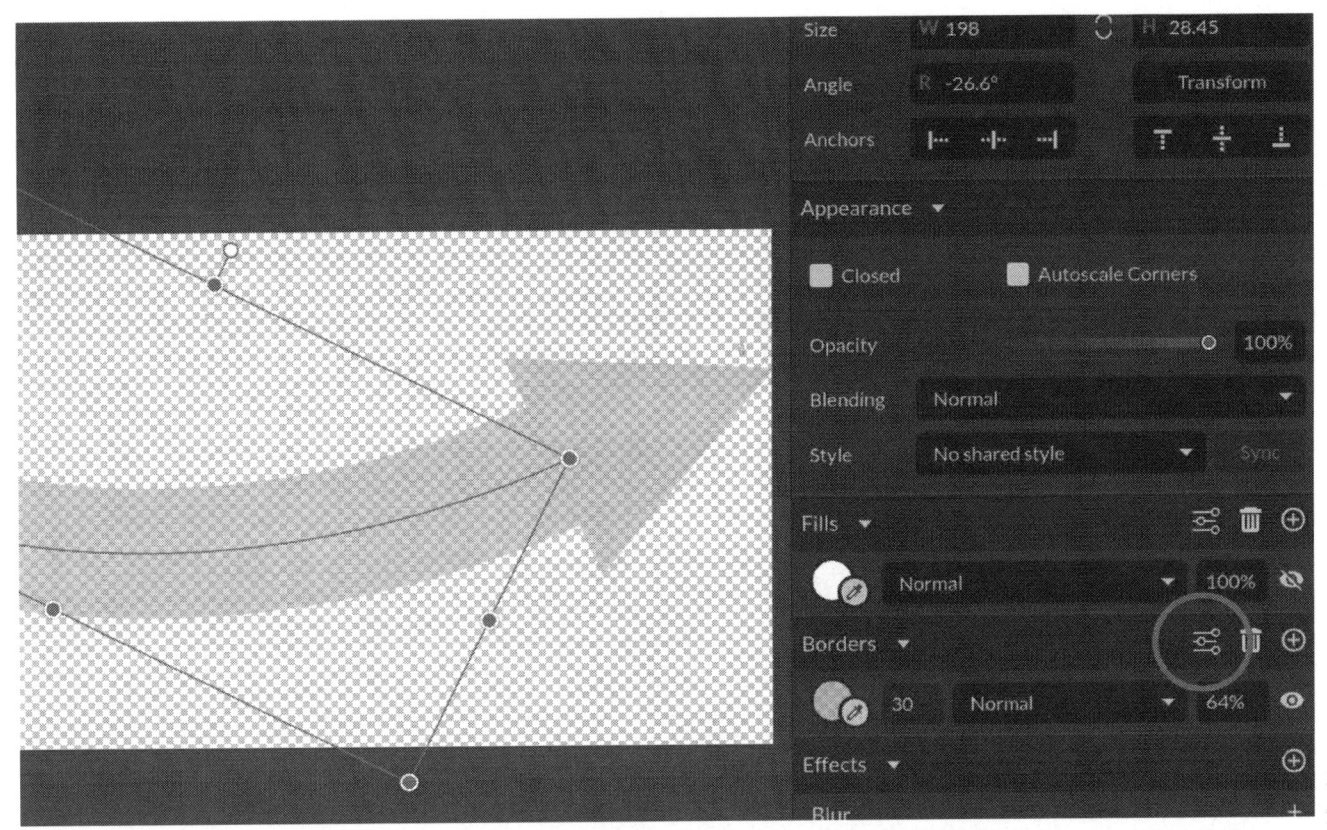

Gravit Designer calls its strokes **borders**. *Whatever*, Gravit Designer. On this panel, you can change the color of the stroke by clicking on the colored circle under the word 'borders' (arghhh, there it is again) and the width of the stroke by changing the number on the right of the colored circle

The *sliders* icon on the panel (that I've helpfully circled in red) allows you to enter the settings of this particular stroke and change its caps style, as well as add objects at the start and/or end of the stroke. You can also make the path dashed by adding values for the dash width and gap.

Strokes (lines) do not have an important attribute that other shapes have: **fill** and **fill color**. Let's take a look at some other shapes and explore fills in the process.

Rectangles

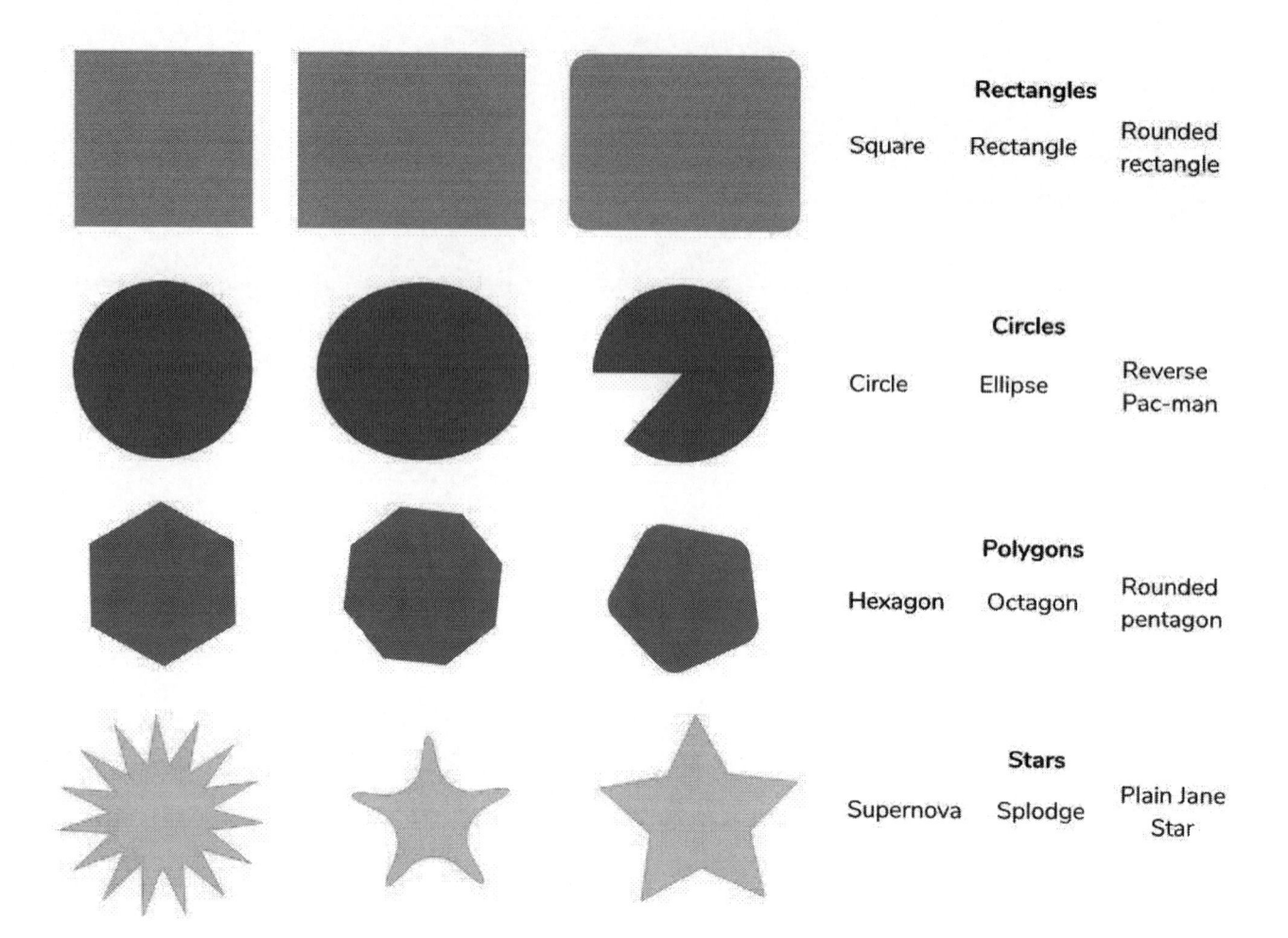

| Square | Rectangle | Rounded rectangle |

Circles

| Circle | Ellipse | Reverse Pac-man |

Polygons

| Hexagon | Octagon | Rounded pentagon |

Stars

| Supernova | Splodge | Plain Jane Star |

Other shapes

An important tip for all filled shapes

Before we study each shape individually, here's something that you need to know: to create regular shapes, like a perfect circle or a square, first hold down the Shift button on your keyboard and then click and drag to create the shape you've selected. After you've created the shape, release the mouse button and *then* the Shift button.

Making shapes

I've already shown you how to select a shape type in Gravit Designer and it's a similar process in all other vector graphics software. Select the Shape tool and then the kind of shape you want to draw. Click on the canvas and drag to make a shape that has the size you want and then release the mouse key. Congratulations — you just created a shape!

Most shapes have their own unique attributes, in addition to some common ones they share. For example, a circle can either be a full circle or have a slice taken out of it, similar to a pie chart. A polygon can have five sides (pentagon) or eight sides (octagon) or any number of sides, really (anygon — OK, I just made this up). A star can have five points like a pentagram or a hundred points. Experimenting with shape attributes is a lot of fun and can lead to happy accidents, so I encourage you to take some time to play around with them .

To find all those shape attributes I keep mentioning, expect to see a **context panel**/menu open as soon as you draw a shape, regardless of what program you're using. In that panel, you'll find all the attributes you can modify. In Gravit Designer, the context panel looks like this, in the case of a circle:

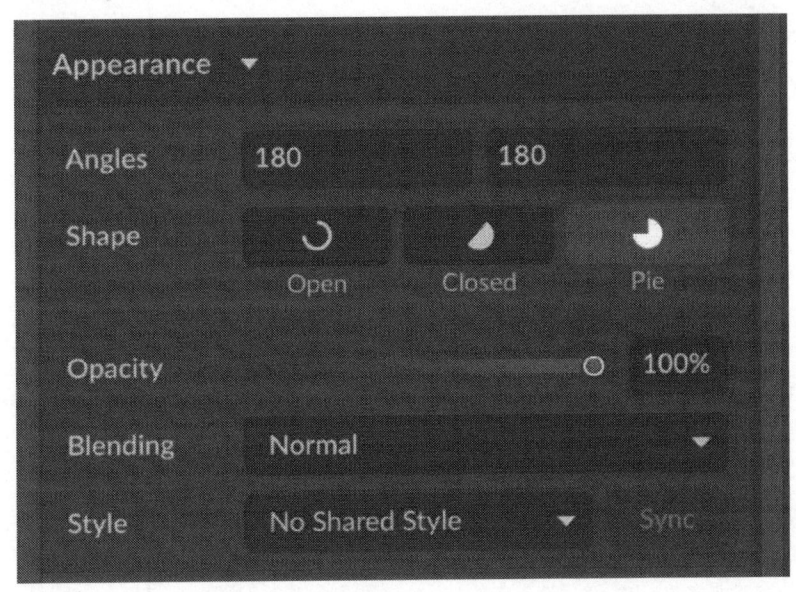

As you can see, it contains mostly ellipse-specific attributes for you to modify. Again, take the time to draw some shapes and play around with their attributes. You may be pleasantly surprised by the results.

Fills & Strokes

Earlier in the chapter, when we discussed lines (strokes) and their attributes, you may remember me mentioning that strokes don't have an attribute all the other shapes have: fills. Indeed, all other shapes can have both a fill *and* a stroke.

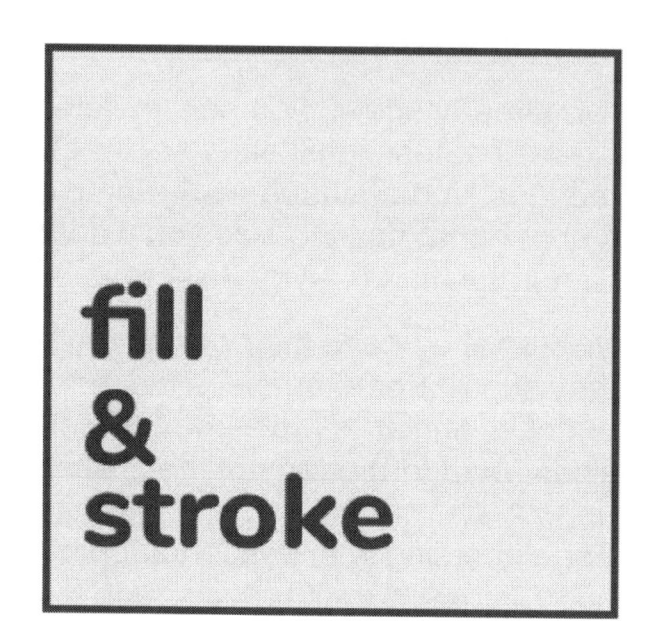

A stroke on a shape can have the same properties as the stroke that follows a path to create a line. For example, you can make the stroke on the rectangle above dashed/dotted:

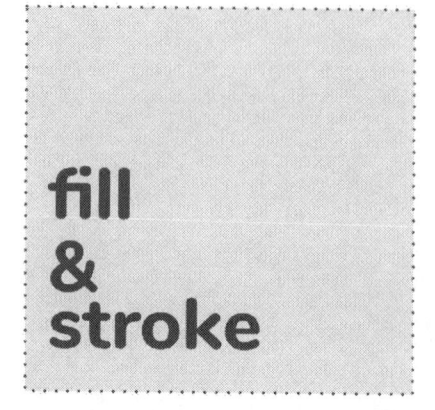

You can also change the stroke color independently of the fill color, apply effects to the stroke, etc.

Now let's examine fills. A shape that has a stroke but not a fill is essentially transparent, ie. if you place it over another shape, you'll be able to see the other shape through it. In the following example, I drew a purple circle and then placed a rectangle I created over the circle.

Rectangle with no fill drawn over a circle

Rectangle with white fill drawn over a circle

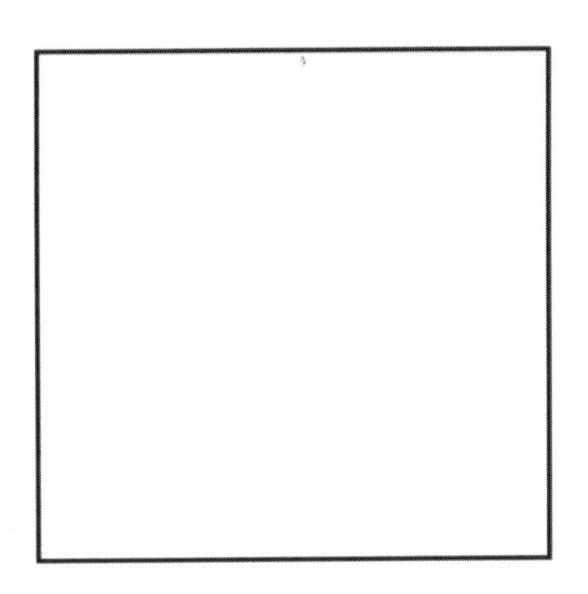

On the left, the circle is visible behind the rectangle, since it has no fill. On the right, the rectangle has a white fill, so you cannot see the circle behind it. But watch what happens when I change the opacity of the rectangle from 100% to 75%

The shape becomes semi-transparent and the circle becomes visible. Notice that in this case, I changed the opacity value of the entire square shape (from its context panel AKA Appearance panel in Gravit Designer, as shown before) so the stroke of the rectangle became dimmer too. The opacity values of the stroke and the fill can also be adjusted independently of each other, in their respective panels (Borders and Fills panels, as shown below)

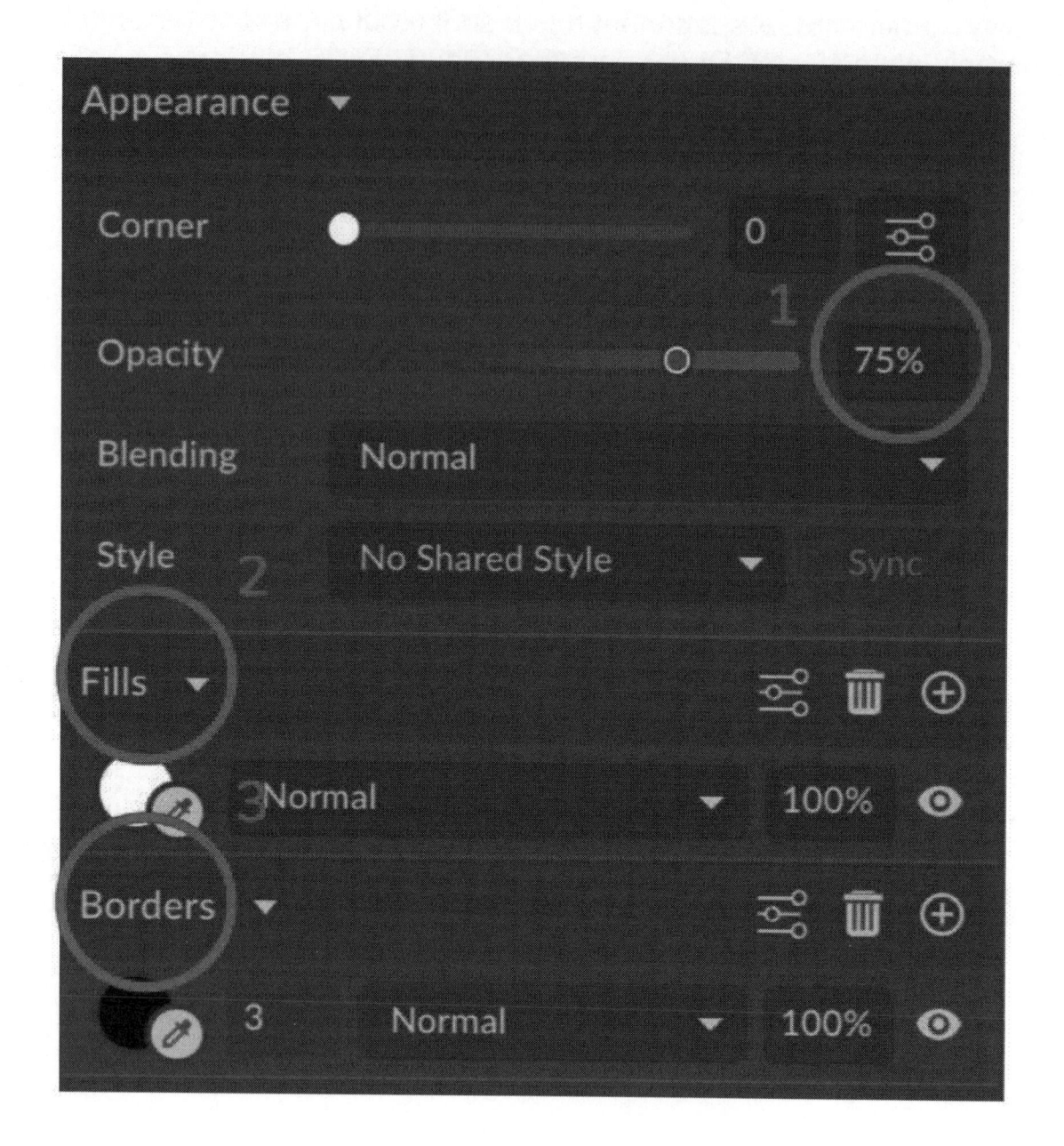

On this panel above, I've marked the entire shape's opacity adjustment section as **1**. I've also marked the Fills section, where you can make adjustments to the shape's fill as **2**. I also marked the Borders section as **3**.

Just to make some things clearer, I'll explain what's going on in this panel in some detail.

In the Fills section, you can add a fill to the shape you've selected by clicking the "+" button. If the shape had no fill when it was created, this will add its first fill. If it already had a fill, this will place another fill on top of the first. The second fill will cover the first fill, rendering the original fill invisible. "Then what's the point?" you may ask. I know. I ask myself the same thing every day.

But enough introspection. The point is this: check out the subsection in the Fills section that currently says "Normal". That's the **blending mode** and, while a discussion of blending modes is outside the scope of this book, you should know that some blending modes (of which there are many) will mix the various layered fills in such a way as to make the ones in the back visible. This is the reason you can add many fills to the same shape.

On the right of the blending mode dropdown, there's a percentage that currently says 100%. That's the **opacity value** of the selected fill. If you reduce the value, the shape's fill will start becoming translucent, revealing what's behind the shape. If you drop it to 0%, and its the only fill the shape has, the shape's fill will become transparent. However, as I've already mentioned, this won't affect the stroke of the shape at all, if such a stroke exists.

Next to the opacity value, there's an eye. That turns the fill's **visibility** on and off.

On the Fills panel, you'll also see a trash can icon and a sliders icon. The trash can icon deletes the selected fill (to select a fill, simply click somewhere on the fill's panel where you won't hit anything else). The sliders icon sets the fill rule, which you shouldn't concern yourself with.

We've already discussed the Borders panel in the Line section so I won't bore you (or myself) by repeating what I said. I'll just add that, like you can do with fills, you can apply multiple strokes of different widths to the same shape, which can make for some funky stylings!

In this example, I didn't use any fills just a circle with three different strokes, each with a different color and width. Here's the Borders panel for this circle. I'll show you how to do the slanted text effect later.

Gradients

Finally, let's talk about gradients. A gradient refers to the (usually) smooth transition of one color into another, although a more correct but less practical definition would be color variance based on position. On our 'Funky!' badge above, the center of the stroke was a bit too empty and plain, so I used a **radial gradient** as the fill of the circle. Here is the result:

As you can see, the central part of the fill is white but it fades into a warm orange as it moves outwards toward the circumference of the circle.

Shortly after the 80s, gradients fell out of fashion faster than hair metal but they've made a (welcome, in my opinion) return lately, as the high-res displays we're using these days make them look much smoother and less horribly dithered.

There are three main types of gradient

- **Linear gradient**: the color changes across a straight line
- **Radial gradient**: the color changes across the radius of a circle
- **Angular gradient**: the color changes following the rotation of the radius of a circle

This explains it more clearly:

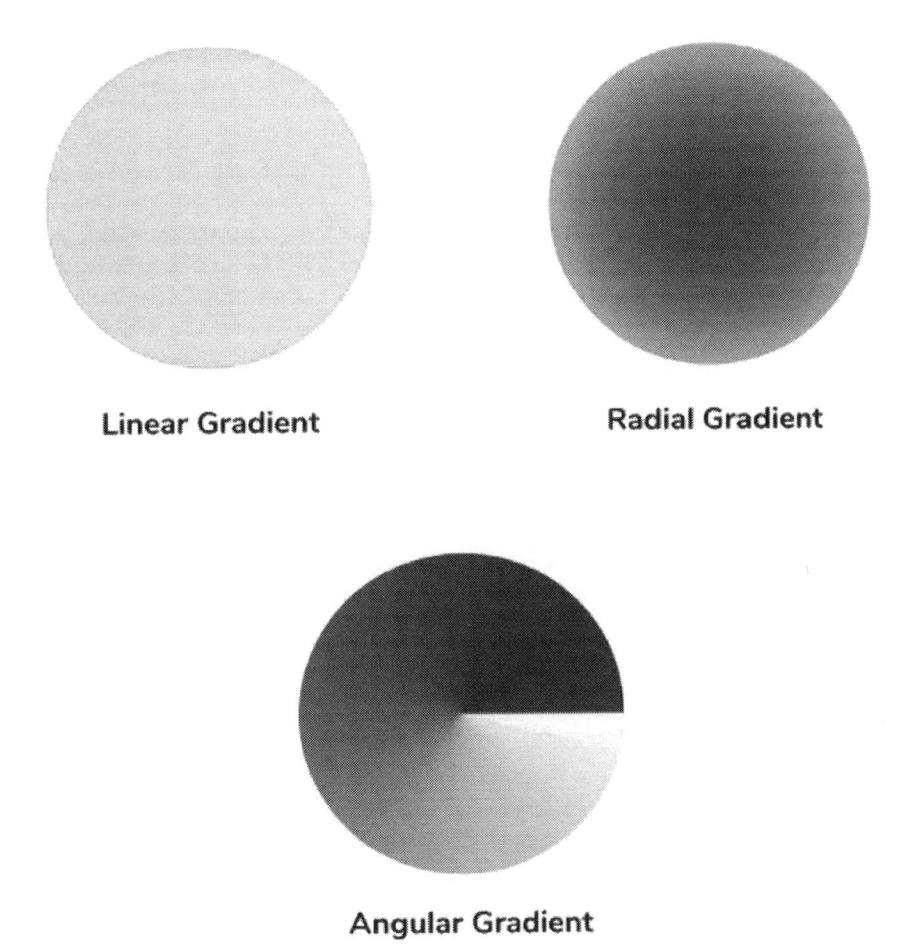

Linear Gradient

Radial Gradient

Angular Gradient

In the case of a linear gradient, you can change the direction of the gradient by rotating a helpful affordance that appears whenever you apply the gradient.

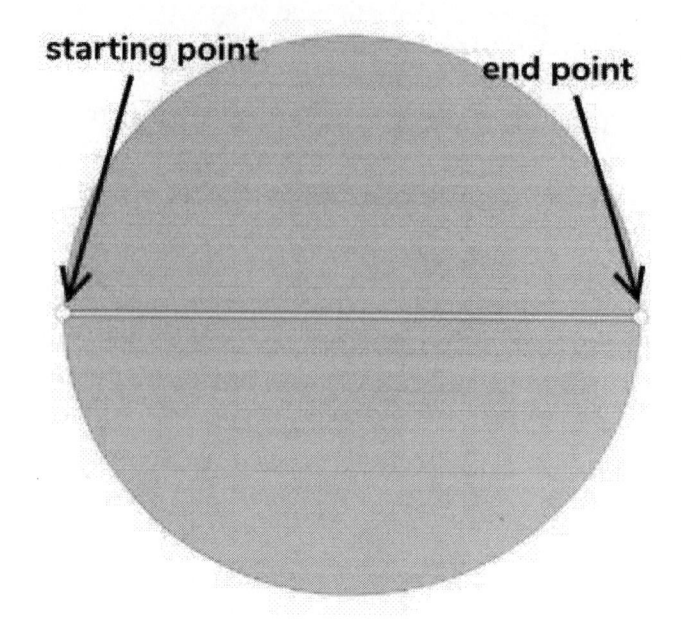

The gradient affordance has a starting point and an endpoint. By clicking on either of those points, a panel will appear that will let you change the starting color and/or the ending color of your gradient. Clicking somewhere in between the points will add a third (and a fourth, should you click again and so on) color point. This means that **a gradient doesn't have to be limited to two colors**. You can change between as many as you want.

You can also rotate the affordance of a linear gradient, thus changing the direction of the gradient too. Simply click and hold on the starting or ending points of the affordance and drag.

Finally, gradients can also be applied to strokes and (with an intermediate step I'll explain later in the "Working with text" chapter) to text.

GRADIENT ON TEXT!

Gradient on a stroke

One last tip, before we move on to an example of an icon created with primitive shapes and your exercises for this chapter: **gradients work great with noise and halftone effects**. As these types of effects tend to make gradients look less sterile and help them come alive. Here's a sunset illustration I created in five minutes using just shapes, gradients and the Noise, Blur and Halftone effects, followed by a quick explanation of how I achieved said illustration.

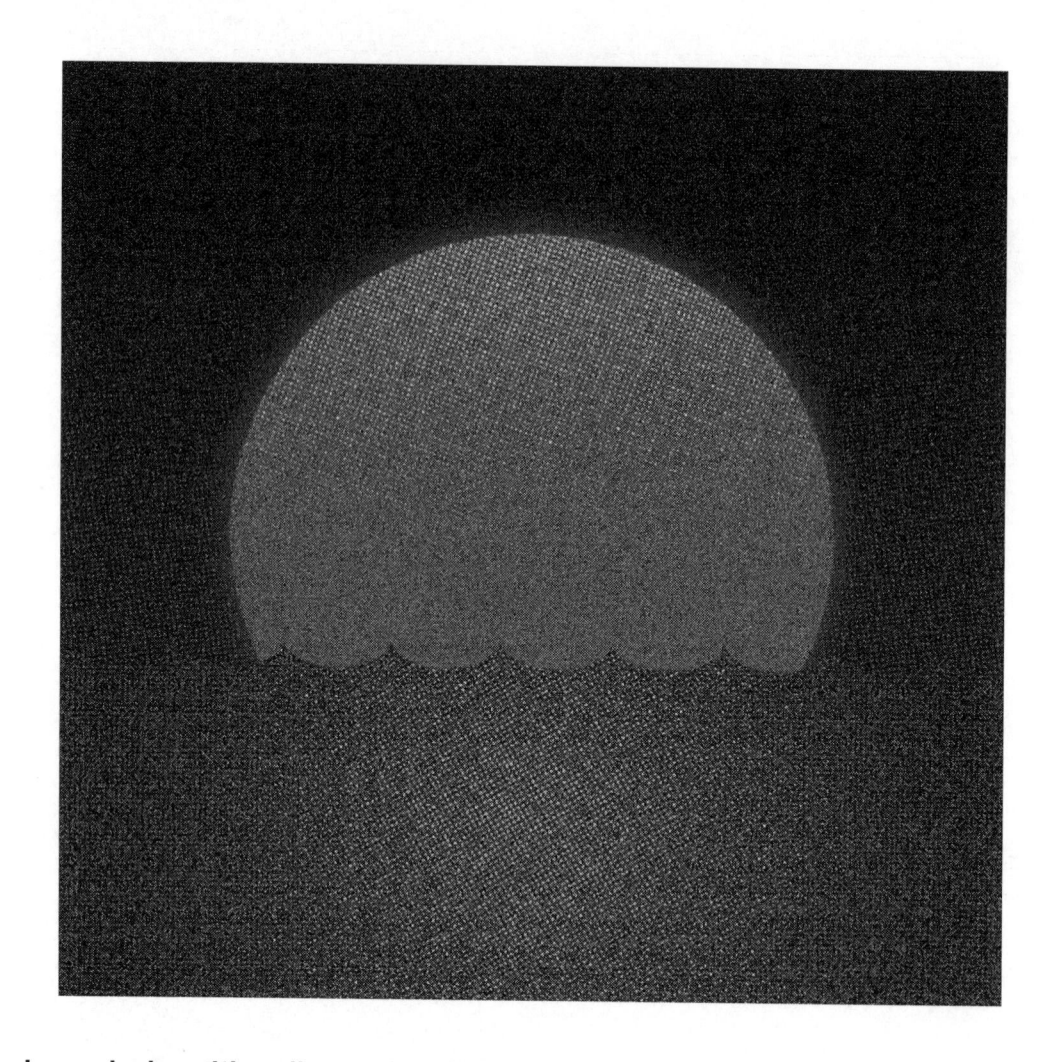

The sun is a circle with a linear gradient applied to it, starting with orange at the top and ending with purple at the bottom. The sky is simply a rectangle behind the sun, with a linear gradient from top to bottom, with black as the starting color and deep purple as the ending color. The ocean is again just a rectangle in front of the sun (the waves were created using boolean operations, which is the subject of the next chapter, so don't worry — we'll get there soon!) with a radial gradient, starting with blue at the centre and fading into a deep purple at the periphery. This gives the illusion that the ocean is being illuminated by the setting sun.

All of the objects have been heavily treated with the halftone and noise effects. To give the sun its glow, I duplicated it and moved the copy behind the original sun. I then applied A LOT of blur to the copy, which made it disperse outwards and gave it the appearance of glow. If I wanted to create more papercraft-like illustration, adding a drop shadow effect to the ocean would help a lot. More about effects in the—you guessed it—Effects chapter.

You can see the result of adding a drop shadow on the ocean below:

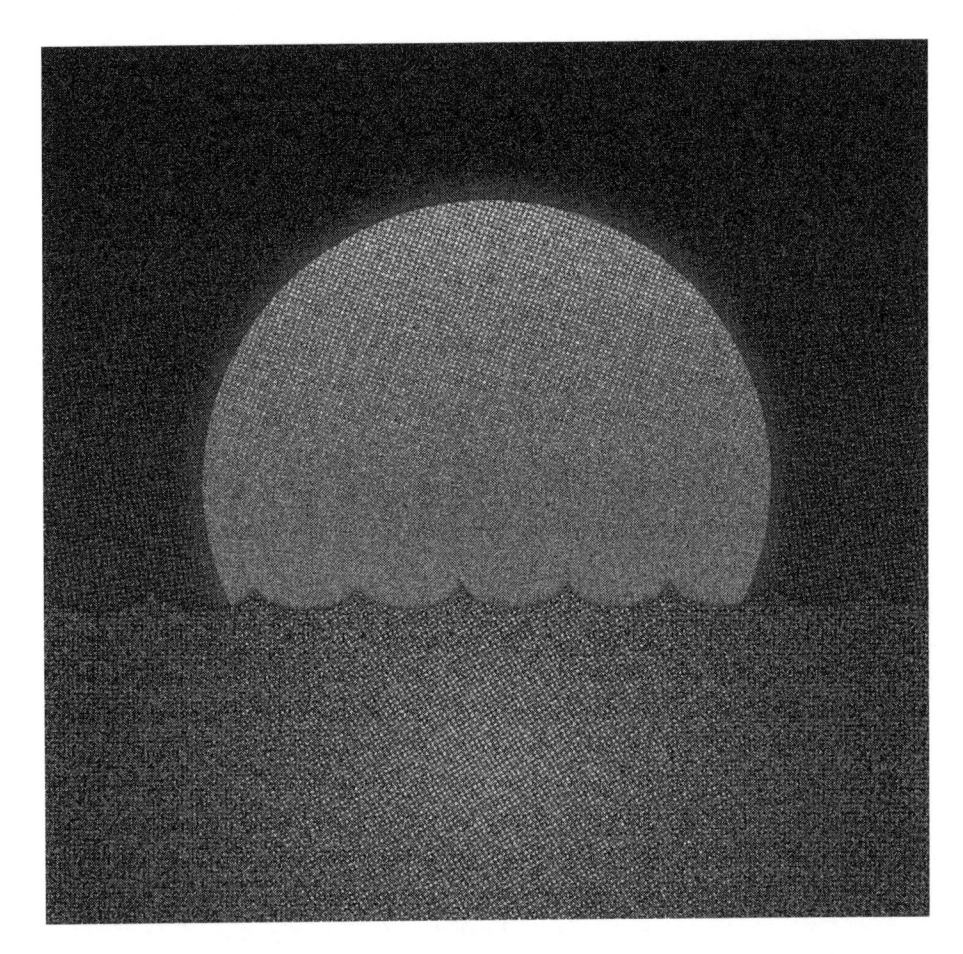

You may still have one question left for me to answer: "What do you mean when you say that you moved this rectangle in front of the sun and the other rectangle behind the sun?" Don't worry, all will be explained in the chapter about z-ordering.

A folder icon example

This is a folder icon I created using only rounded rectangles and a single boolean operation. In order to show you how I made it, below the icon itself I've added the **Outline view** of the icon. To access the Outline view in Gravit Designer go to **View > Outline View.** The outline view in a vector graphics program shows you the outlines of your shapes (Captain Obvious Strikes Again!) without any fills or stroke attributes. Think of it as the architectural plan behind the illustration itself.

[Folder icon illustration]

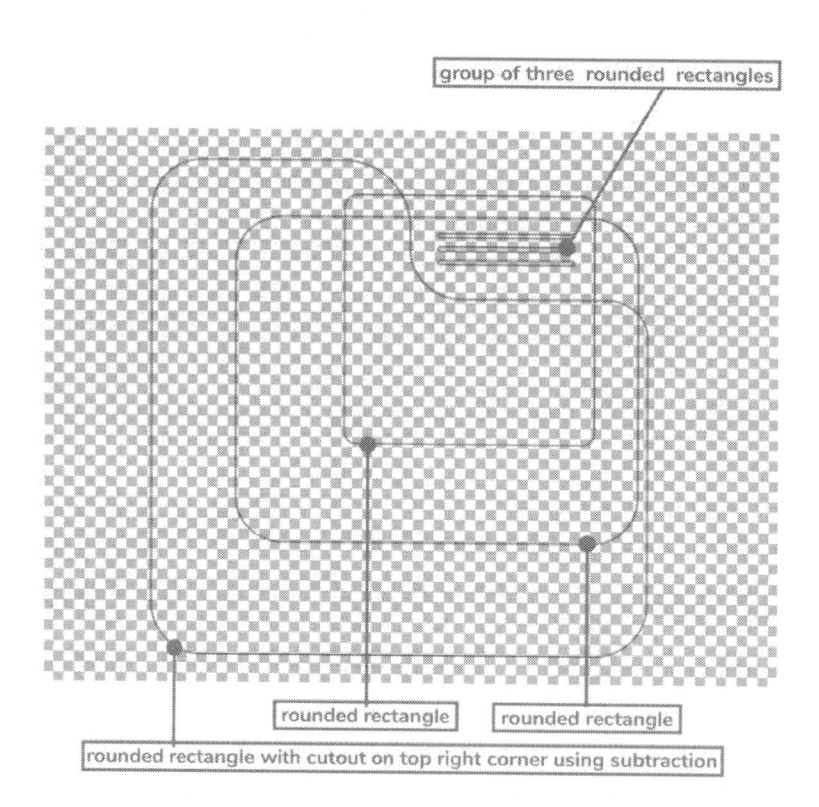

[Diagram showing construction with labels:]
- group of three rounded rectangles
- rounded rectangle
- rounded rectangle
- rounded rectangle with cutout on top right corner using subtraction

The entire thing is comprised of six rounded rectangles with fills in a particular back-to-front configuration. One of the six rectangles is missing a piece on the upper right corner. Study it carefully because as you'll find out, you can make all sorts of simple icons and logos by layering shapes on top of each other.

If you're worried about how you'll stack the shapes in the order you want or how you'll remove a piece from a shape, rest assured that those skills are very simple to learn in a matter of minutes. You'll just have to wait until their respective chapters, **z-ordering** and **boolean operations**, to learn how to do it.

Primitive Shapes: Chapter exercises

Exercise 1: Freestylin'
For this first exercise, I want you to just open your software, create a new project (**File > New**) and start playing around with shapes and their attributes. Make some rounded rectangles, a few perfect circles and draw some lines.

Exercise 2: Create a simple tennis racket
With what you've learned in this chapter, create a simple tennis or ping-pong racket. You don't have to add any detail.

Chapter 5: Layering with Z-Order

What's z-ordering?

Z-ordering may sound like something a nuclear physicist would do at a particle accelerator facility but it's probably the easiest concept to grasp in this book.

But what exactly does it mean?

Your screen is a two-dimensional surface, so if you draw something in one part of the screen and then draw something else that shares that part of the screen with the first object, one of these things has to happen: either the first object drawn will (fully or partially) cover the second one or the second object drawn will (again, fully or partially, depending on size and location) cover the first. What actually happens in this case is that **the second object is drawn over the first object**. If you draw a third object, that object will be placed in front of the other two and if you draw a fourth object, that one will be placed in front of the other three and so on and so forth.

You may remember from high school math that when creating the axes of a graph, the horizontal axis is usually dubbed the X-axis and the vertical axis is dubbed the Y-axis. Since we live in three-dimensional space, there's a third axis that instead of up/down (Y) or left/right (X) refers to **back/front**. That axis is called the **Z-axis**. This is why the order in which objects are placed on screen (back to front by default) is called Z-ordering.

For most people, this makes intuitive sense. Somehow, if you ask people with no experience in computer graphics which object will cover which, most of them will assume that the second one will be drawn over the first one—at least in my experience.

Knowing what Z-ordering is means that you are now a Knight of the Order of Z. Congratulations! Your helmet will arrive shortly in the mail. It's quite heavy, so we had to charge you a bit extra for shipping.

Modifying the z-order of objects

Let's say that you've drawn two objects that overlap, like so

The rectangle was drawn first, so it sits in the back like a loser while the circle was drawn second, so it sits in front of the rectangle, all smug and shit. But, oops—you didn't mean to do that! Instead, you want the rectangle to come to the front, leaving the circle in the back. There has to be a way to do this, right? Surprisingly, there is not.

Just kidding—*of course there is*! In fact, every single vector graphics software gives you a very simple way to do it. Since this is a fundamental skill to have, I'll show you how to do it in all three (Adobe Illustrator, Affinity Designer & Gravit Designer) I use. In all of them, you **select the object you want to move** to the back or to the front and

- **In Adobe Illustrator**, you go to Object > Arrange > Bring Forward or Object > Arrange > Send Backward
- **In Affinity Designer**, you go to Layer > Arrange > Forward One or Layer > Arrange > Back One
- **In Gravit Designer**, you go to Modify > Arrange > Bring Forward or Modify > Arrange > Send Backward

There are alternate ways to move objects in the z-axis in all of these programs. All of them have icons in their toolbars or certain panels that, after selecting the object you want to move, let you move it simply by clicking the "forward one" or "backward one" button. Gravit Designer's look like this

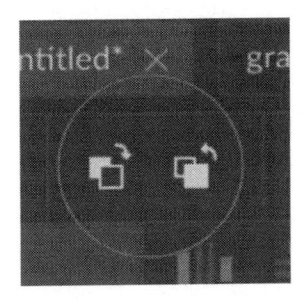

Yet another way to do the same thing is to use the Layers panel in any of the programs. There, you'll be able to drag and drop entire layers or specific objects, thereby rearranging them on the z-axis. The Layers panel in all programs look extremely similar. This is how the Layers panel looks in Gravit Designer

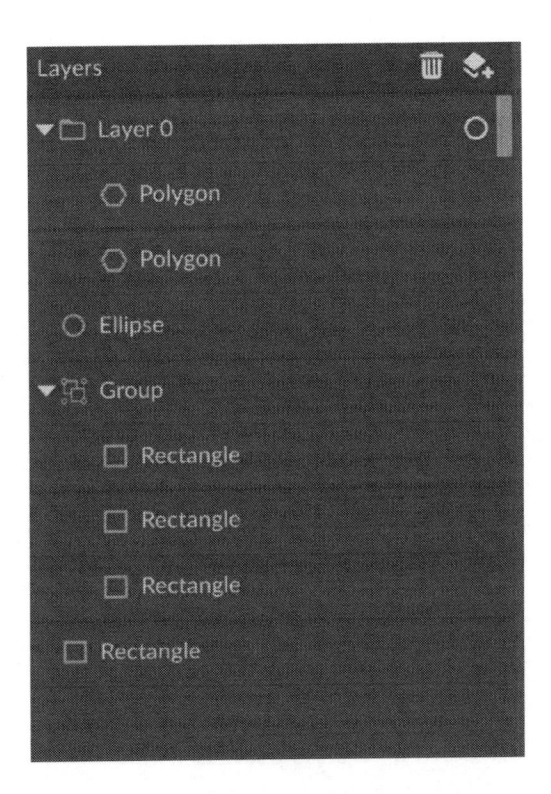

Starting from the bottom of the list, you have the object that's the furthest back, ie. the one that all other objects, groups of objects or layers on the list are in front of. That's the lone 'Rectangle' object. Higher on the list, you'll find something called a Group, which contains three 'Rectangle' objects. The objects in this group are in front of the lone 'Rectangle' object that's lower on the list. Next, there's a lone 'Ellipse' object, which is in front of the Group I just mentioned. Finally, there's a 'Layer 0' object that's in front of the rest of the objects in the panel, which contains two 'Polygon' objects.

Here are the most important operations you can perform on this panel:

- As I've already mentioned, you can drag and drop objects to change their z-order in the hierarchy. For example, you can bring the bottommost Rectangle object to the front of the rest of the objects by dragging and dropping it to the top of the list.
- You can drag and drop objects in groups or layers.
- You can delete objects by selecting them and clicking the trash can icon
- You can create new layers by clicking the layers icon that sits to the right of the trash can icon

One question I get very often is this: **what's the difference between layers and groups?** For all intents and purposes, they are interchangeable. Their difference is mostly contextual: if I'm creating an object that's comprised of smaller sub-objects (a car, for example), I'll create a Group that contains the various car parts (wheels, chassis, windows, etc.)

On the other hand, if I want to manage the stacking order of an illustration's levels, I'll usually use a layer. For example, if a person is on the same plane as the car, I'll include the car group and the person in the same layer, unless there's a good reason not to.

But really: don't stress about it. Use whatever makes the most sense to you.

At this point, it would probably be a good idea to mention the keyboard shortcut for grouping and ungrouping objects, as it's something you'll be doing very often. First, select the objects you want to group together by holding down Shift and clicking on the objects you want to select. This is how you select multiple objects. Keep in mind that you'll have to use the Select tool for this to work, which looks exactly like a mouse pointer. Then, on a PC, press **Ctrl+G**. On a Mac, the shortcut is **Command+G**.

Practical z-ordering tips

When you're placing objects on the z-axis, think of how an object that's further back will look like. Objects that are away from us look smaller than objects that are nearer. They also look darker and (sometimes) fainter. If you want to make your illustrations more lifelike, don't forget these tips.

I'll use the sunset & ocean illustration I posted earlier in the book as an example of this. Let's say that only one layer of sea and waves (ie. the way it currently is) is not enough. We need to add two more. An easy way to do that would be to copy and paste (Ctrl+C/Command+C followed by Ctrl+V/Command+V) the waves object twice and move each copy lower in the illustration. The result would be something like this:

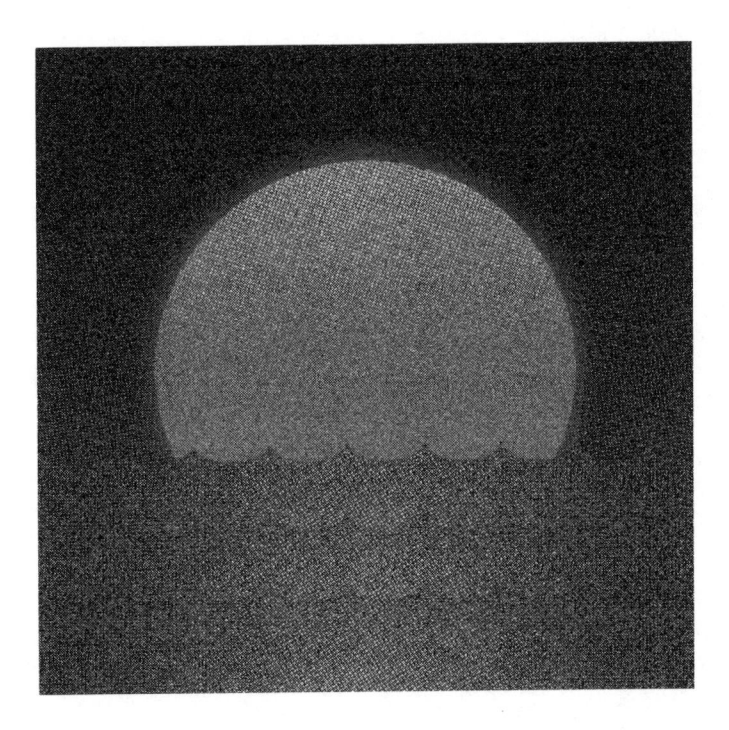

Not bad, but what happens if you select each copy of the waves and change their brightness slightly, so that the one on the back is the least bright, with the one in front of it being slightly brighter and with the one in the front being the brightest (changing the brightness is something you'll learn how to do in the Effects chapter)? Then we get something like this:

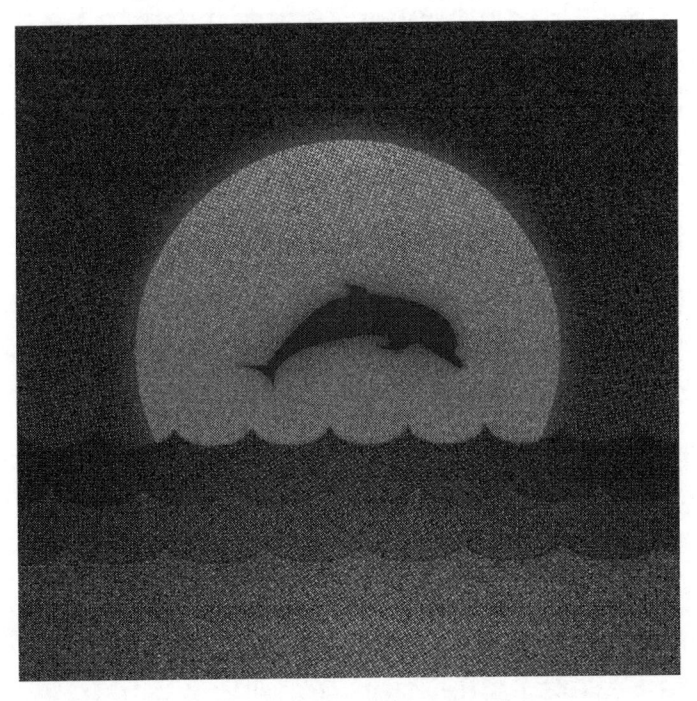

I think you'll agree that this looks much better! And, hey—I added a dolphin! Dolphins make everything better.

Here's another example I shat out in a minute to illustrate this point. Keep in mind that the filename of the exported .jpg was *crappy mountain.jpg* and adjust your expectations accordingly:

I'm pretty sure than, even with this level of shartistry on display, you'll easily be able to tell which mountain range is supposed to be in the front and which one is supposed to be in the back. Obviously, since the light grey mountain range is partially obstructing the darker mountain range, it has to be at the front. However, darkening and adding some slight blur to the mountain range in the back helps with the illusion of depth.

Z-ordering: Chapter exercises

This is going to be a simple one: create a new project and draw a lot of shapes on the canvas. Then, start altering their z-ordering, bringing some of the shapes to the front and sending others backward.

Optionally, create a new layer and, with the layer selected, start drawing shapes on the canvas again. Take a look at the layers panel, under the layer you have selected. What do you see?

Multiselect some other shapes by holding down Shift and clicking on them. Then group them together by pressing Ctrl/Command+G on your keyboard. With the group selected in the Layers panel, start drawing shapes on the canvas. Take a look at the group that has been created in the layers panel. What do you see now?

Chapter 6: The Power of Boolean Operations

What are boolean operations?

Welcome to my favorite part of the vector graphics creation process! I'm sure you're going to love it.

Here's a figure showing a list of the most commonly-performed boolean operations. Before I go on to explain what boolean operations actually are and what they do (and also, most importantly, how we can use them in practice), try to figure out what's going on on your own.

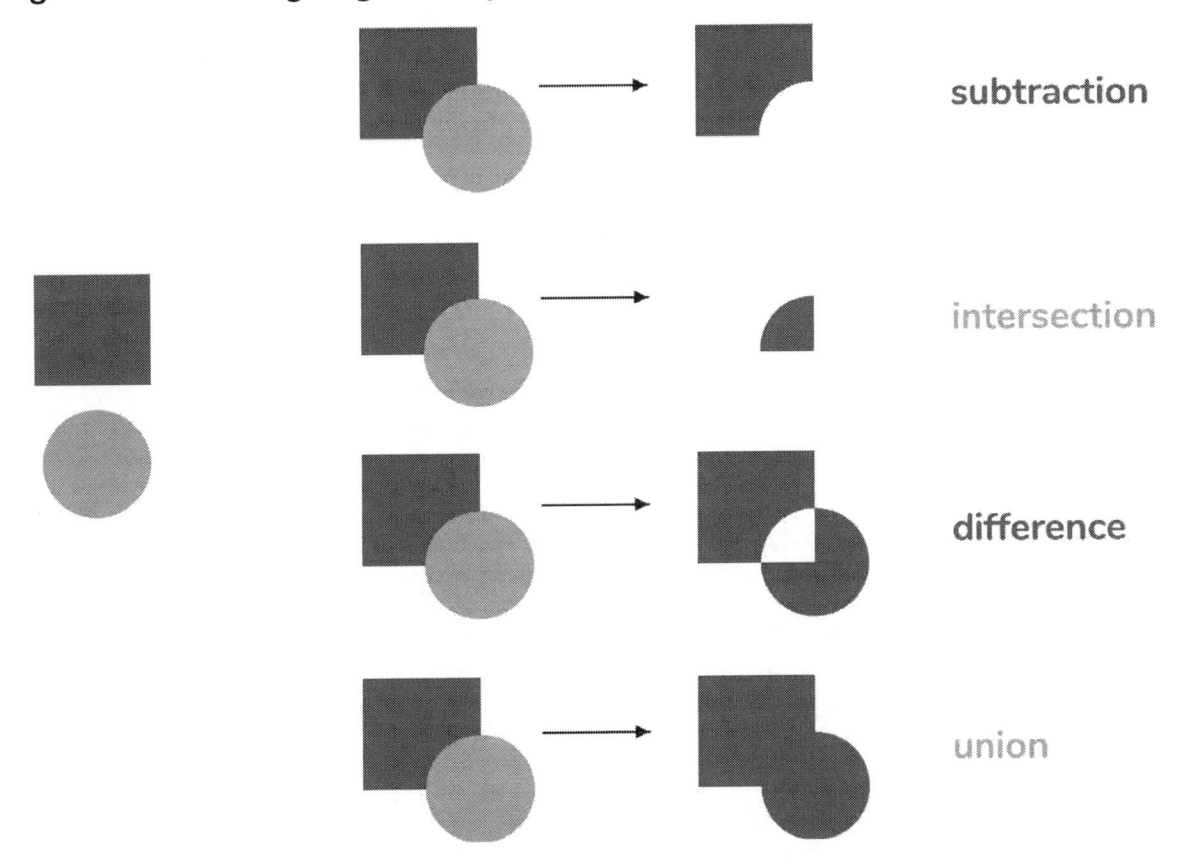

subtraction

intersection

difference

union

It looks so very technical and boring. If you wanted to do math you wouldn't have dropped out of elementary school, right?

WRONG.

With the god-like power of boolean operations in your hands, the sky's the limit. By now, you must have guessed that boolean operations allow you to perform operations that affect multiple shapes in a variety of ways.

Subtraction will take two (or more) overlapping objects and remove the sections that overlap from the object in the back, while eliminating the object in the front completely. The important thing to remember (and something that comes pretty intuitively to most people, honestly) is that **the object in the front removes a piece from the object in the back** — not the other way around. In the example above, the circle is clearly in front of the rectangle, so the circle "bit out" a piece of the circle.

Intersection keeps only the parts of the shapes that overlap (intersect), which makes it the opposite of subtraction, ie. it keeps only the parts that the subtraction operation would remove. Some might say that subtraction and intersection are two sides of the same coin, the yin and the yang, if you will. I won't, because that's pretty fucking lame. There's one more thing I want you to notice in this operation: the result of the intersection operation (the little slice of circle that remains) **has inherited the color of the object in the back** — not the one in the front.

Difference will remove the parts of the objects that overlap but will keep the rest of the objects untouched. Again, notice how **both objects have inherited the color of the object in the back**.

Union will unite the shapes. Man, Captain Obvious is really killing it in this section. Once more, the resulting shape inherits the color of the object in the back.

Many people have wondered what will happen if you try to perform boolean operations on objects that don't overlap. On June 12th, 2016, researchers at the CERN institute tried to do just that. The result was a barely-containable black hole that threatened to bring about the gravitational collapse of the Earth. Thankfully, they were able to avert the disaster with the help of Peter Higgs (who was, at the time, Skyping instructions from the toilet) and some WD-40.

Oh, you wanted a non-ridiculous answer? Sorry: the actual answer is that a **subtraction** operation will eliminate the object in the front without affecting the object in the back (since the object in the front acts like a destructible eraser that has nothing, in this case, to erase), an **intersection** operation will make both objects disappear (since they don't intersect anywhere), a **difference** operation will keep the objects as they are (since they don't overlap, they are *all* difference) and a **union** operation will unite the objects into a compound shape but keep the distance between them unaffected.

See? If you think about it, it all makes sense. But enough theory! Let's go do some (reversible) damage to some shapes.

Performing boolean operations

Start practicing by creating a new project (the resolution you use doesn't really matter, although in projects with lower resolutions everything will work faster—that includes boolean operations, transformations, effects, etc.)

After you've created the project, draw two shapes on the canvas (what kind of shapes you draw is irrelevant, as long as they aren't lines) and, using the selection tool (the tool that looks like a mouse cursor), place them so that they partially overlap by dragging them in position. You should have something that looks kinda like this

Now **select both shapes** (either by holding down Shift and clicking on the first and then on the second shape or by drawing a rectangle that contains both shapes with your selection tool).

After you've selected both objects, they will be highlighted by a **bounding box**. The bounding box is a rectangle that surrounds a selection and allows you to perform operations such as translation, rotation, etc. on the selected objects. More on this box in the chapter on Transformations. Here's what the selection and its bounding box should look like

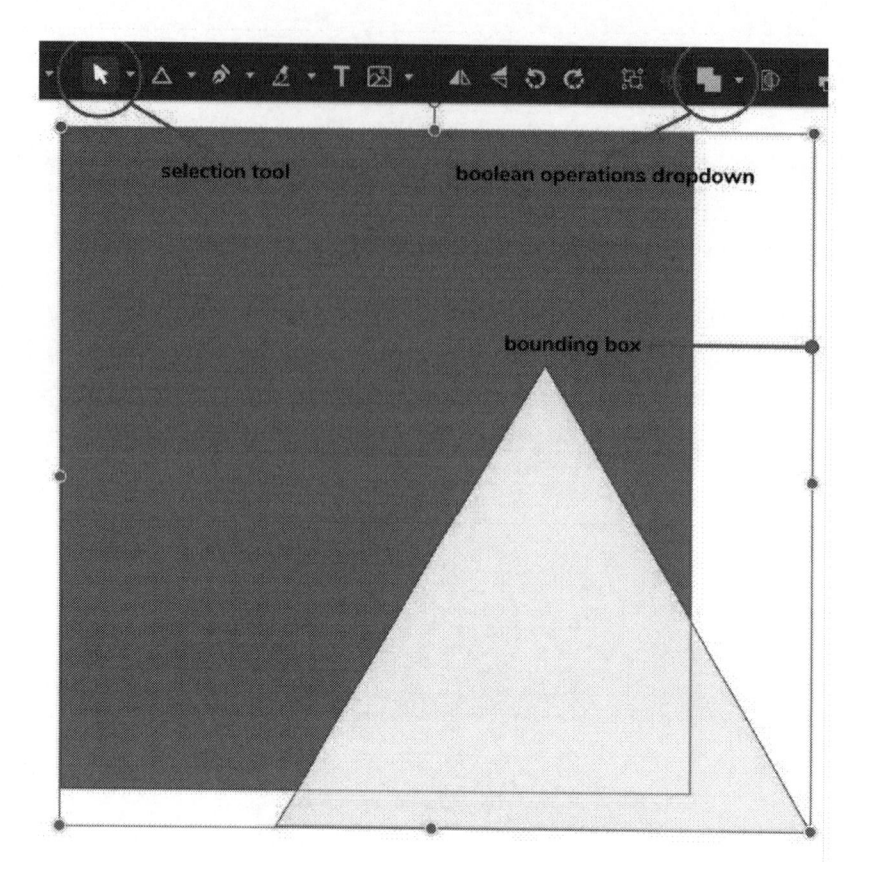

The picture above points out the selection tool, the bounding box and the boolean operations dropdown on the toolbar.

Now that both objects are selected, perform the boolean operation by selecting it from the dropdown in your toolbar. I'll go with subtraction:

If you're using Gravit Designer, click on the resulting shape with your selection tool and select **Modify > Path > Convert to Path** from the menu. This will convert the resulting object into a pure path, instead of the weird chimera state of rectangle-with-some-triangle-subtracted that Gravit Designer likes to keep the results of boolean operations in. That state has its place, since it will allow you to move the pre-operation shapes around freely, updating the result in real time. However, converting the result into a pure path creates a new object and stops the software from treating the shape as a **compound shape** (a shape that's comprised of two or more basic shapes), which makes things much simpler and reduces the possibility of weird behavior in the future.

Practical applications of boolean operations, with examples

In this chapter's example illustrations, I'll be showing you how to create a crescent moon, the waves I used for the sunset over the sea illustrations, a cloud, the folder icon from the chapter on shapes and an outline lightbulb icon. Sit tight, things are about to get interesting!

Creating a crescent moon

Let's start with the easiest one. Trying to create a crescent moon without using this method is highly advised against and also probably a violation of the Geneva convention.

Start by creating two perfect circles of the same or different size. Something like this:

Now partially cover one circle with the other by moving them around with your selection tool. You can do this in a variety of ways, depending on the thinness of the crescent you're going for and perhaps the required cartoonishness. Right now, I'm going for something like this:

Now, select both circles (Shift+click on each circle or include them both in a rectangle drawn with your selection tool). If you've selected them correctly, a bounding box will appear around them.

With the circles selected, go on your toolbar, click the boolean operations dropdown and select **Subtract**. Success!

Now would be an awesome time to select the resulting crescent and go to **Modify > Path > Convert to Path.**

Let's play around a little. Right now, the object is only fill. Let's remove the fill (remember how to do that?) and add a border:

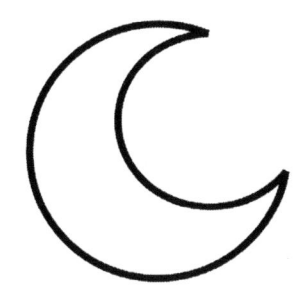

Very cool, right? You now have an outline icon and it took you five seconds (hopefully) to do it! If it didn't take you five seconds, go back to the Shapes chapter and re-read it.

Since we've created an outline icon, I should probably mention this: if you're creating an icon set with outline icons, make sure that you keep the stroke/border size consistent between all icons. Nothing screams *amateur* more than an icon set with inconsistent stroke sizes.

Creating the waves

Before you read any further, and taking into account the method we used to create the crescent moon, take a minute to think about how you would go about creating the waves.

Minute over? Let's see if we agree.

First, create a wide rectangle. Make it turquoise. Now create a small circle and make multiple copies. To do this, select the circle and use the shortcuts

Ctrl/Command+C and **Ctrl/Command-V** multiple times; in Gravit Designer, the copy/pasted shapes are placed over the original shape, so don't be surprised if you don't see the copies. They are there, just start dragging each copy away with your selection tool.

Here's what I did:

Now start dragging each copy of the circle with your selection tool and place it next to each other so that they cover the rectangle like so:

It doesn't have to be perfect, but try to get the circles touching tangentially and keep them centered relative to each other on the Y-axis.

I bet you know what I'm doing next! Select everything (easiest way is **Ctrl/Command+A**) and, from the boolean operations dropdown select **Subtract**.

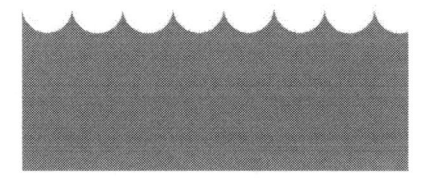

Neat, huh? Now select **Modify > Path > Convert to Path** again.

Now would be a good time to mention that I've had an advantage over you all this time. No, not my stunning looks and winning personality, although probably that too. My advantage was using the **Snapping** tool. The snapping tool is on your toolbar and it looks like a magnet:

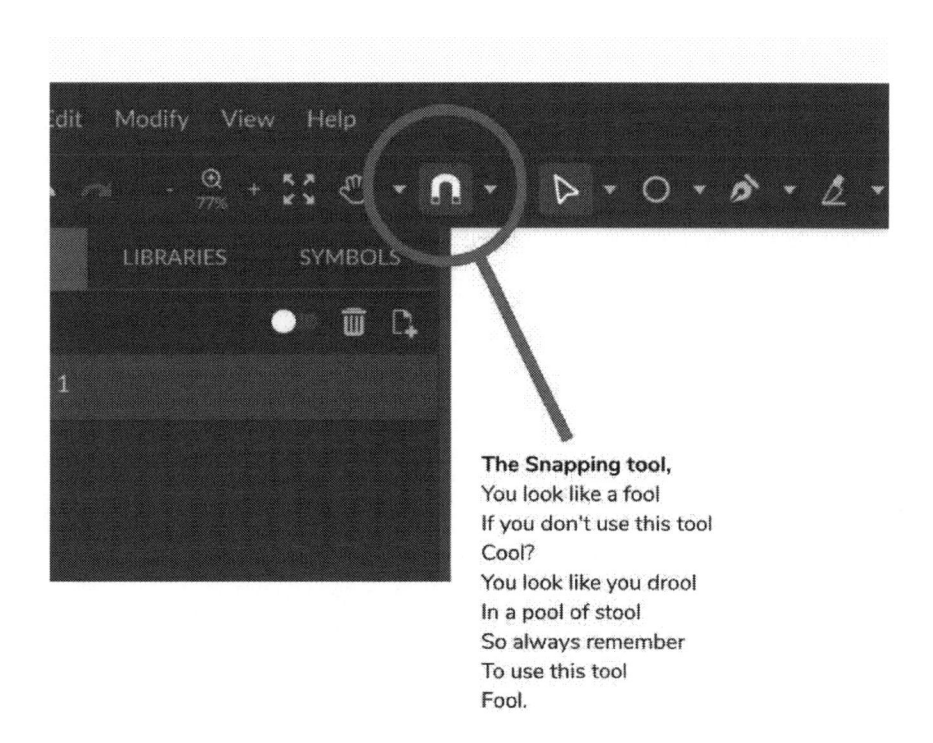

The Snapping tool,
You look like a fool
If you don't use this tool
Cool?
You look like you drool
In a pool of stool
So always remember
To use this tool
Fool.

The snapping tool is so amazing, I wrote a rap about it. But what does it do?

If you enable snapping by clicking the magnet icon, all kinds of wonderful things happen:

- You get **guide lines**. Guide lines are amazing because they appear when you need them the most. For example, when I was placing the circles next to each other in the waves example, two kinds of guide lines appeared: whenever a circle came in contact with another circle, a line would appear as if to say "the circles are touching now, that's enough!" The other kind of guide line appeared whenever I was moving a circle in the Y-axis. Whenever neighboring circles' centers or baselines were aligned in the Y-axis, I would get a line indicating that. This essentially means that the shapes are snapping to each other, guiding you with their placement.
- The shapes **snap to the grid**. The grid is an actual grid of lines that help you place items in a harmonious manner on your canvas. Usually, and by default, the grid is invisible but still there. With snap disabled, you can move your shapes freely, without any apparent stepping. Enabling snapping means that your shapes' movements are constrained to the grid. This may sound limiting but it actually helps to achieve tidy results, especially if you're designing user interfaces.

Creating a cloud

We've only been using subtraction so far, so let's use some union too. Create two perfect circles and a rounded rectangle on your canvas. To create the rounded rectangle, simply draw a normal rectangle and in the shape's appearance/attributes panel, increase the value of the Corner attribute. I took it to the max.

You should have something like this

You can now place them in such a way that a cloud will be formed. I came up with this but you can do your own thing:

Select all the shapes and from the boolean operations dropdown select Union. Don't forget to go to **Modify > Path > Convert to Path**.

If you cannot place the various shapes in a configuration that you find pleasing, go to **View > Outline View.** The outline view is perfect for placing objects relative to each other, especially when said objects are ellipses. Once you're done, disable the outline view by following the same steps.

To practice, embellish the cloud project by adding the sky and the sun peeking behind the cloud (go through the Z-ordering chapter again if you forgot how to do this). Also, copy and paste the cloud and create a couple of smaller ones to place around the canvas. You should end up with something like this:

Creating the outline lightbulb icon

Let me start this example off by showing you the final icon

Think about this icon: what are its component parts?
If you answered 'a circle and two rounded rectangles', congratulations.

Let me break this down for you. Here are the parts I used individually:

Bringing these parts together, using the Union boolean operation, removing the fill and adding a stroke (border) results in the finished icon I showed you.

Boolean Operations: Chapter exercises

In this chapter's exercise, you must combine everything you've learned about primitive shapes, z-ordering and boolean operations to recreate the folder icon I showed you in the Shapes chapter:

If you want, you can go back to that chapter and take a look at the outline view with explanation I have provided. However, try to do this on your own. The result doesn't have to be exactly the same but try to get as close as possible.

If you're stuck or need any other kind of assistance while you're creating it, send me an email at sebastian212000@gmail.com. I'd be happy to help!

Optional exercises:

1. Create a cloud and make an outline version of it. Bonus points if you add some rain!
2. Create Pac-Man and then make an outline version too.

Chapter 7: Art of Transformation

OK, I admit it: transformations are boring. I am, of course, referring to transformations in vector graphics — not actual, real-life transformations, like that of a lowly caterpillar into a magnificent butterfly or that of an 18-wheeler into a gigantic battle robot from outer space voiced by Peter Cullen.

Transformations in vector graphics refer to the various size-, position- and shape-related operations you can perform on objects, like

- Moving them on the canvas, which is called **translation**
- Making them bigger or smaller, which is called **scaling**
- Rotating them around one or more axes, which is called—unsurprisingly—**rotation**
- Flipping them around, which is called **flippettyflips**. *Fine*, it's not called flippettyflips—but it should be. It's called **reflection**.

Adjacent to these kinds of transformations are things like **alignment** and **distribution,** so both of these things will also be analysed in this chapter.

Despite their fancy names, none of these concepts are difficult to grasp, but mastering them can make a real difference to the quality of your work.

Translation

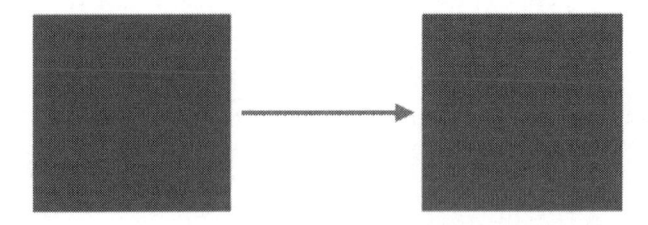

This is an easy one: **translation** refers to the movement of an object from one position to another. The result of translation is a change in **position**.

Changing an object's position is really easy: with your selection tool, click on the object and drag & drop it to its new location.

Holding down Shift while you're dragging the object to its new location will move the object fully horizontally or vertically.

You can also move a selected object by using the arrow keys on your keyboard. Holding down Shift while you're doing that will move the object in bigger steps.

Scaling

Scaling refers to a change in an object's **dimensions**.

Scaling an object is almost as trivial as moving an object: select it with your selection tool and the bounding box for the object should appear.

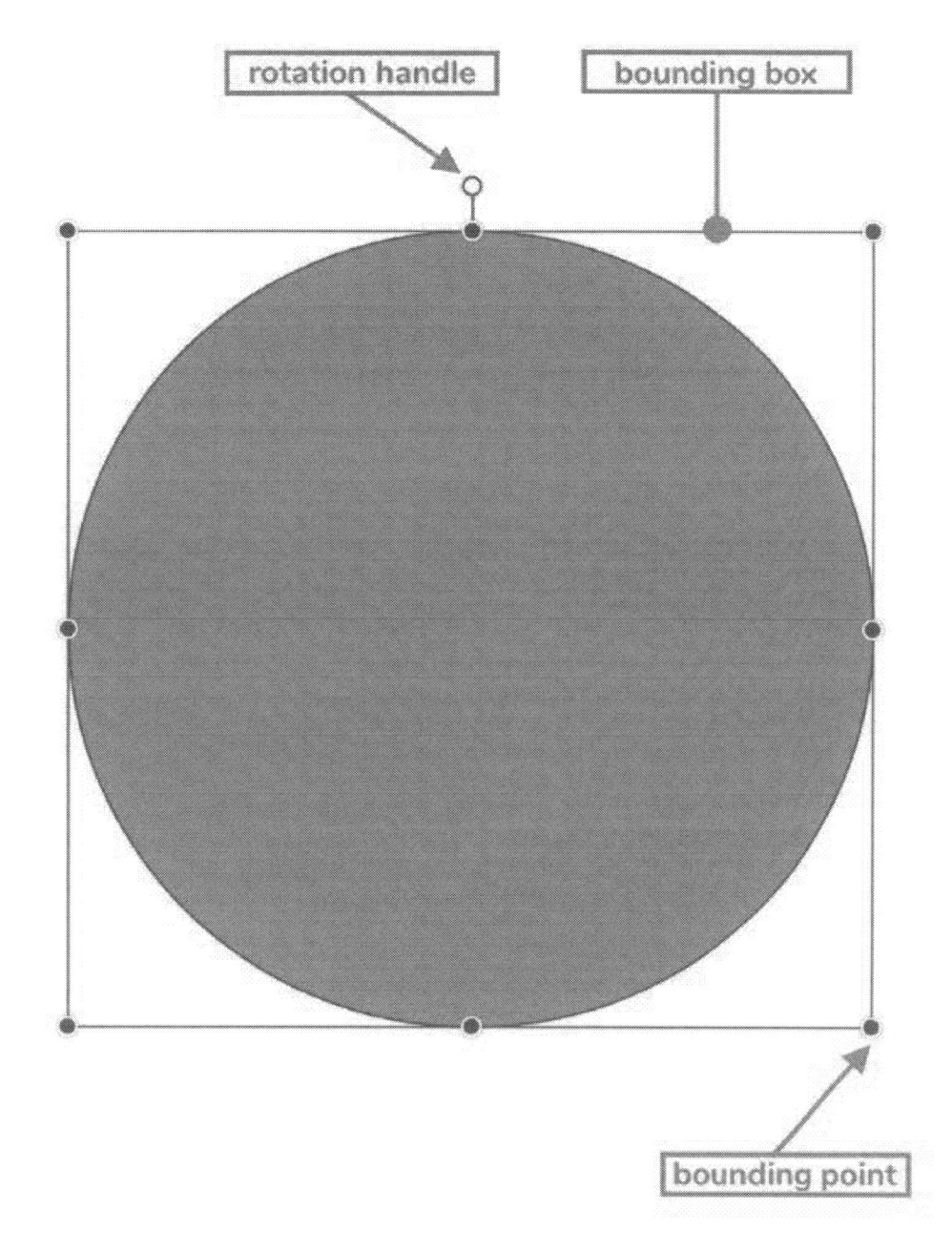

To scale the object, click on one of the bounding points and drag & drop to the preferred size. To keep the scaling **proportionate** (ie. retain an 1:1 relation in both dimensions) hold down Shift while you're dragging and dropping.

Rotation

In the previous figure, you may have noticed something called a **rotation handle**. Clicking that and dragging will let you rotate the object. However, there's another way to do it: if you hover your selection tool near the corner of the bounding box, the cursor will change from the usual arrow to the corner rotation affordance, denoted by a arced line with an arrow on each end, as shown below

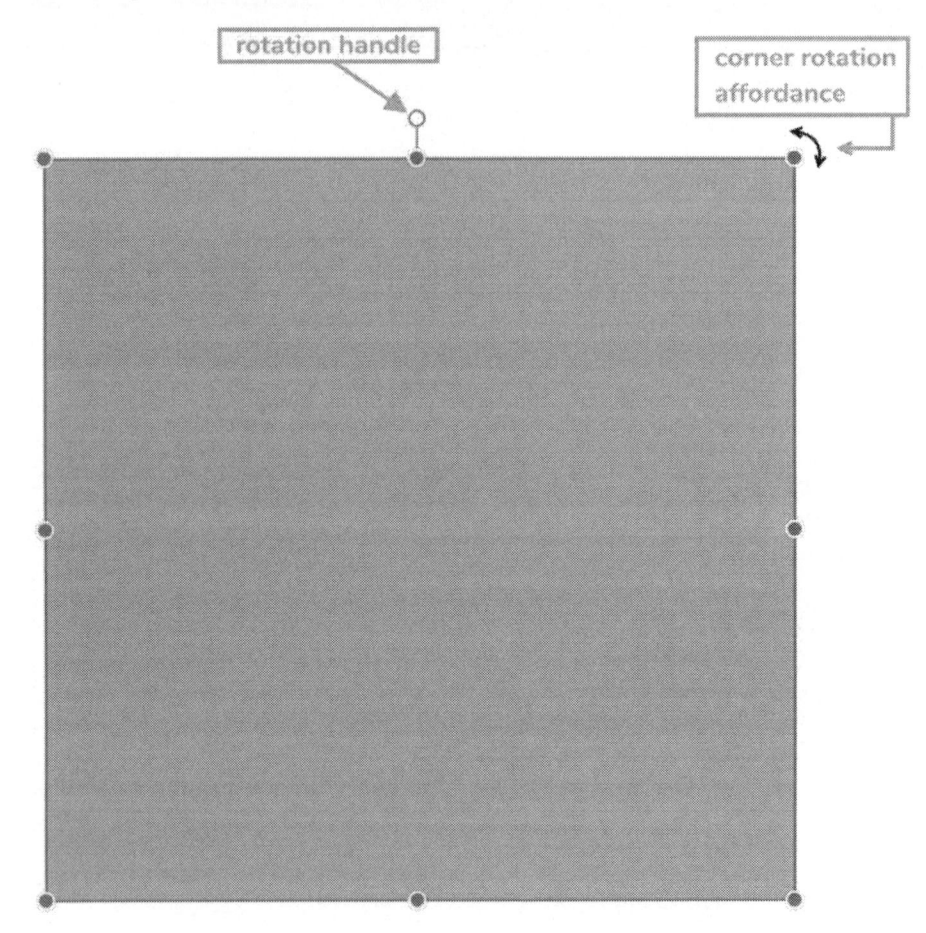

Clicking on the affordance and dragging & dropping also allows you to rotate the object:

Remember that for the affordance to pop up, you first have to select the object so that its bounding box appears.

If you hold down Shift while you're rotating the object, the software will apply the rotation in increments of 45 degrees.

Rotation, unlike what is usually the case with translation and scaling, sometimes requires absolute precision. Sometimes, a rotation of 29.9 degrees won't be precise enough; you'll need it to be 30 degrees *exactly*. To do that, you'll need to use the object's Transform panel, which looks like this

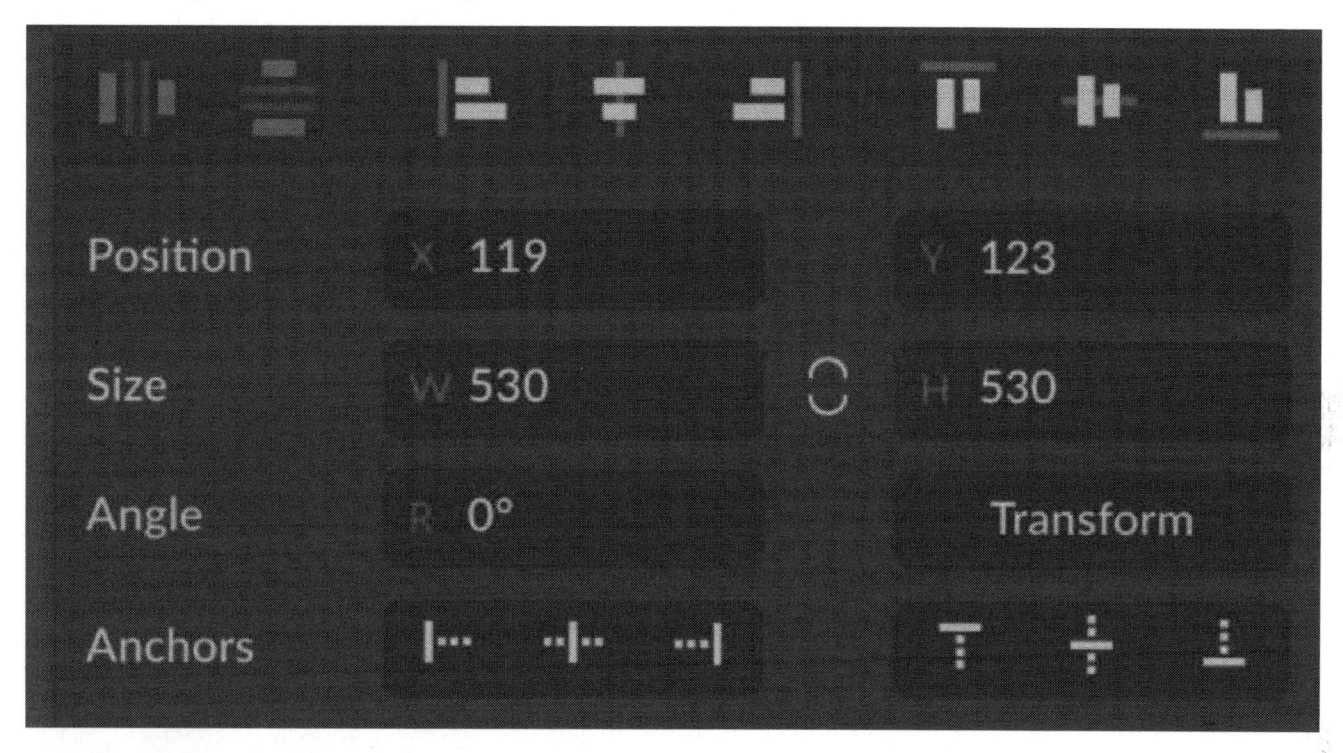

In Gravit Designer, by default this panel appears below the toolbar, on the top right. However, all vector graphics programs have a counterpart to the Transform panel, which usually shows up when you select an object.

As you can see, the Transform panel has a field called 'Angle' into which you can enter a precise value. In Gravit Designer, entering a negative value (eg. -45°) will rotate the object clockwise, while entering a positive value will rotate the object counterclockwise.

Changing the center of rotation

In the transform panel, you'll find a button saying 'Transform'. Clicking this button will reveal some more options but, more importantly, it will place an orange/yellow rhombus in the center of the currently-selected object. That's the

center of rotation for that object. When you start rotating an object, by default it will rotate around an object placed at its center. That's not what you always want.

To change the center of rotation, simply drag it and place it wherever you want, even outside of the shape itself. If you do that, the shape will be orbiting its external center of rotation.

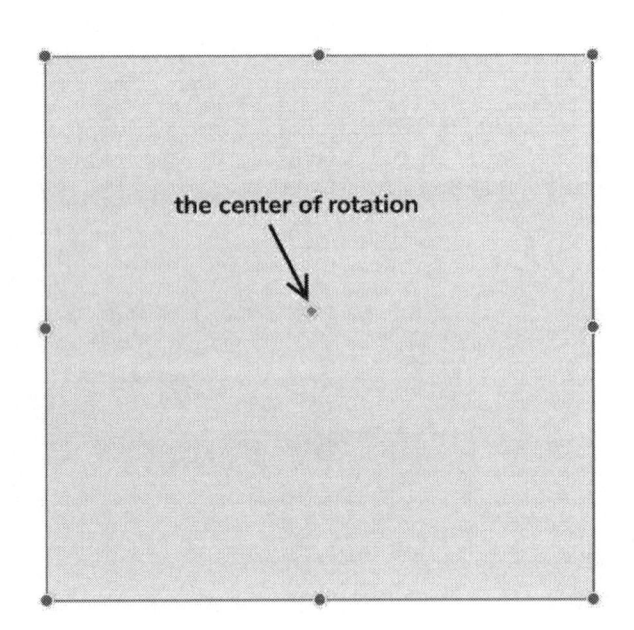

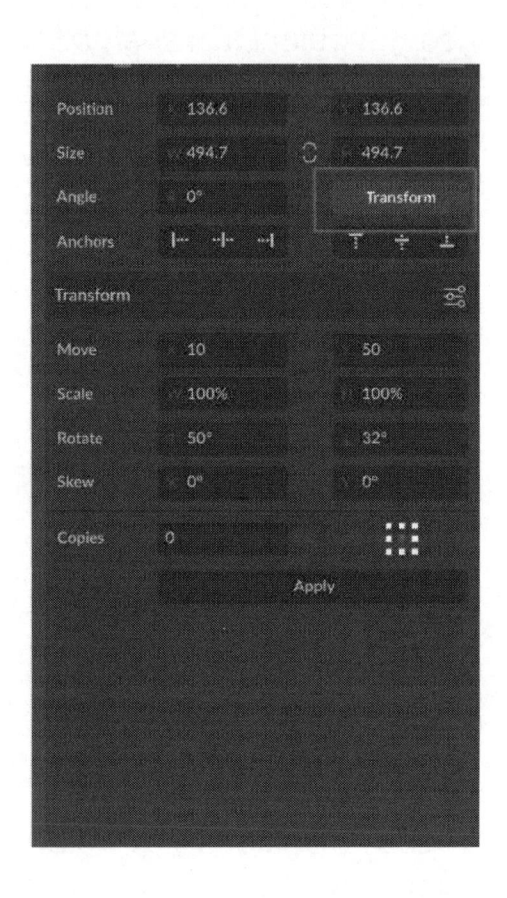

Reflection AKA flippetyflips

Reflection does exactly what it says on the tin: it creates a mirror image of the selected object. Notice that it does *not* copy and flip the copy; it flips the current object. You can flip an object horizontally or vertically, like so:

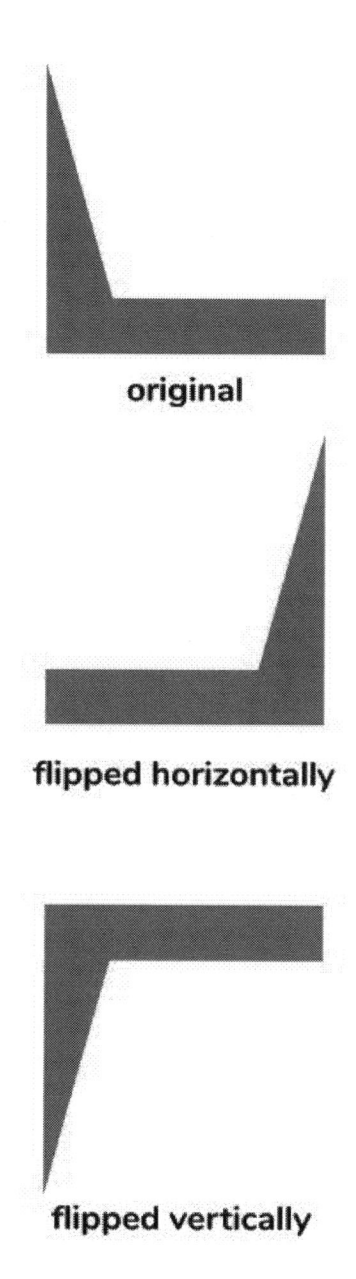

original

flipped horizontally

flipped vertically

The newest question in the long-running "You May Be Thinking…" series in this book may be "Why would I flip an object and not simply create it in the orientation I want it to be to start with?"

Flipping an object is a great way of creating perfectly symmetrical shapes. If you create one half of the entire shape, flip it and then use the Union boolean operation you'll get a perfectly-symmetrical object, faster.

Here's an example:

By now, you should know how to create this shape. In fact, even if you're sure you know, I'd still urge you to sit down and create it as practice. If you're struggling, here's a hint: it involves a triangle, two rectangles, three small squares and the application of subtraction and union. Don't bother with the dots in the shape's fill, that's just the halftone effect I added to make it look old-timey.

I'm now going to copy and flip this shape, so on my computer I'll select the entire shape and then press Ctrl+C (to copy it) and then Ctrl+V (to paste it). Gravit Designer will paste the copy over the original so you may think that nothing has happened, but it's there. To flip the shape horizontally, go to your toolbar and look for these icons:

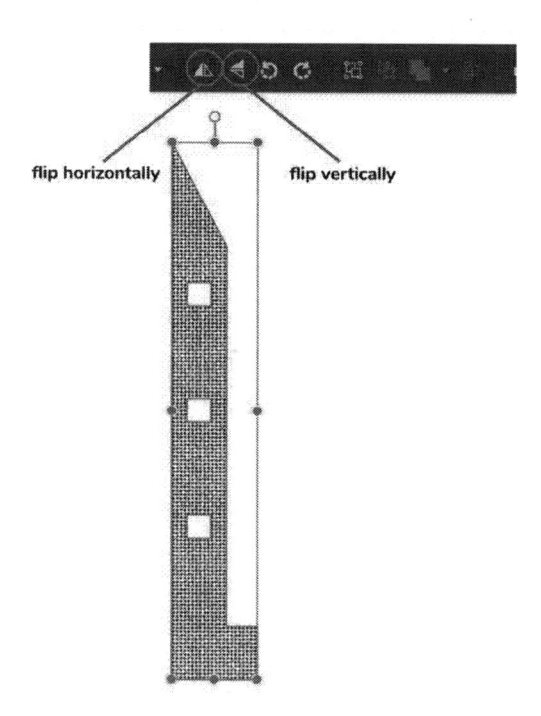

Flipping horizontally will flip the copy (or the original, depending on which one you've selected) and lead to this

...which, if you keep as-is, you could claim that it's three cats on top of each other. Or you could move the flipped copy to the left and have this cool skyscraper graphic:

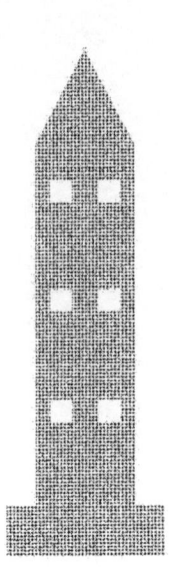

Do whatever you want. I'm not here to tell you how to live your life.

As an aside, if you place an art deco typeface and a nonsense word under the graphic, you can get a nice logo going:

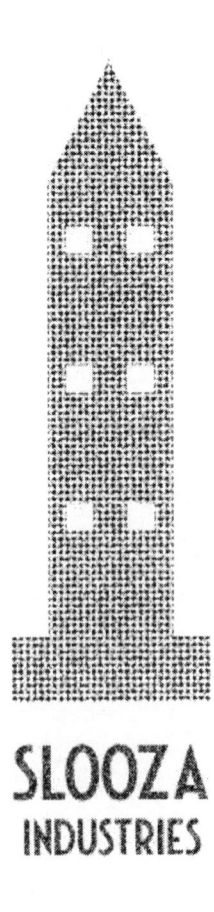

SLOOZA
INDUSTRIES

Alignment

Aligning objects is something you'll be doing very often, especially if you will be doing user interface or any text-related design. Alignment (by definition) always includes two or more objects, so to align your objects you'll need to select them.

Adobe Illustrator, Affinity Designer and Gravit Designer all have their own alignment panels/tools, and they are all pretty much self-explanatory. This is how Gravit Designer's panel looks, with helpful descriptions for each button:

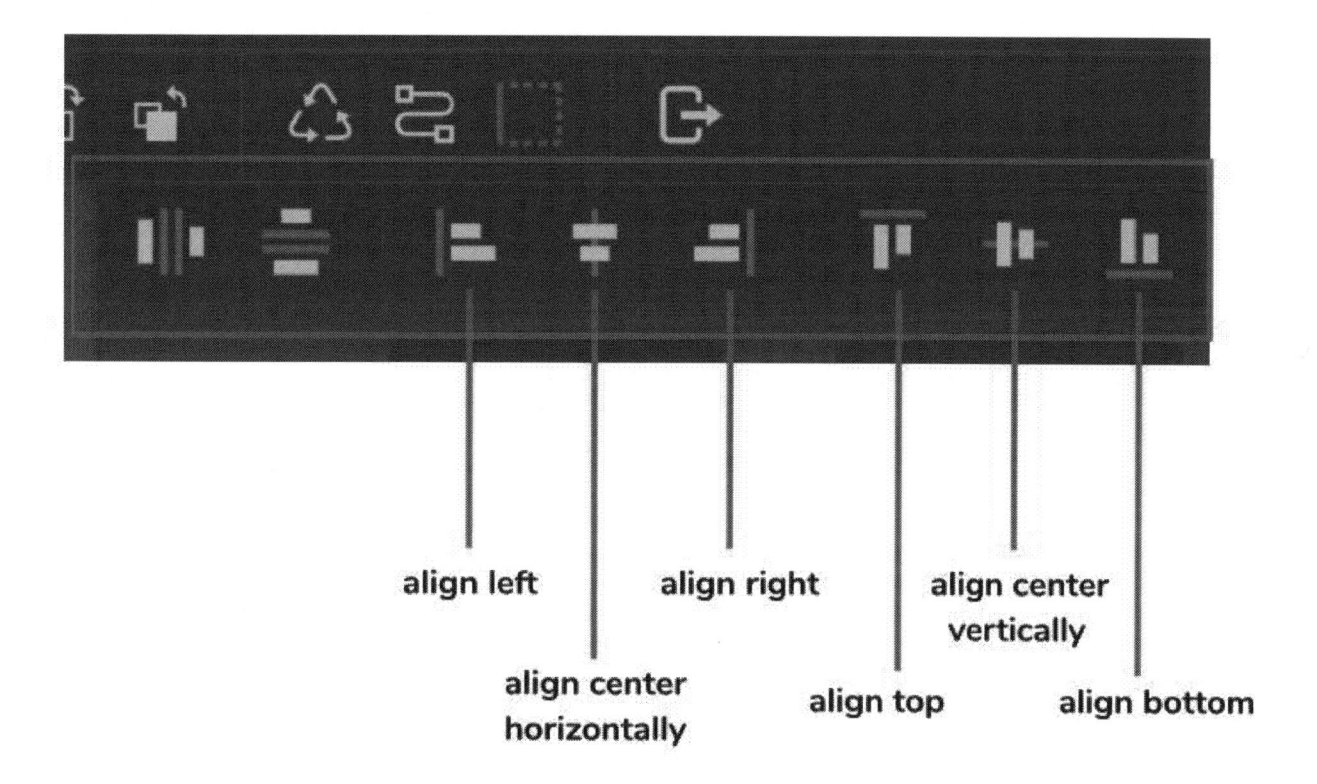

align left — align center horizontally — align right — align top — align center vertically — align bottom

Let's say you have three squares that you've haphazardly thrown on the canvas, hoping that no one will notice. But then someone *does* notice and you have to do something about it:

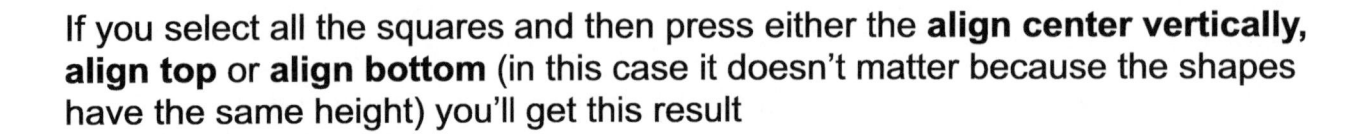

If you select all the squares and then press either the **align center vertically, align top** or **align bottom** (in this case it doesn't matter because the shapes have the same height) you'll get this result

Naturally, if the objects have different heights, it matters what alignment reference you'll use. Here are three unaligned objects

Here's the result for **align center vertically**

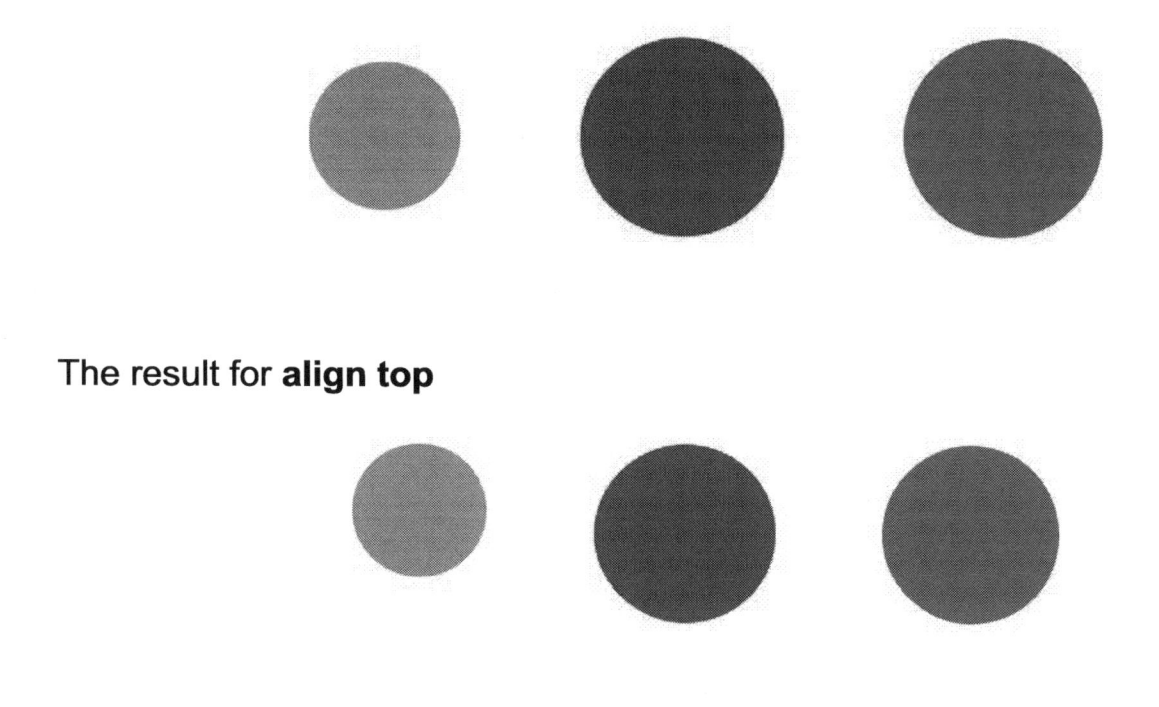

The result for **align top**

And for **align bottom**

Let's also align a block of text with a black rectangle. In this case we'll be aligning the objects left with the **align left** button.

Selecting the black rectangle and the block of text, we press the align left button and the result is this:

DAGON
BY H.P. LOVECRAFT

I AM WRITING THIS UNDER AN APPRECIABLE MENTAL STRAIN, SINCE BY TONIGHT I SHALL BE NO MORE. PENNILESS, AND AT THE END OF MY SUPPLY OF THE DRUG WHICH ALONE MAKES LIFE ENDURABLE, I CAN BEAR THE TORTURE NO LONGER; AND SHALL CAST MYSELF FROM THIS GARRET WINDOW INTO THE SQUALID STREET BELOW. DO NOT THINK FROM MY SLAVERY TO MORPHINE THAT I AM A WEAKLING OR A DEGENERATE. WHEN YOU HAVE READ THESE HASTILY SCRAWLED PAGES YOU MAY GUESS, THOUGH NEVER FULLY REALISE, WHY IT IS THAT I MUST HAVE FORGETFULNESS OR DEATH.

Align functions also work between *groups* of objects. In the following example, we want to center the two blue circles with the orange one.

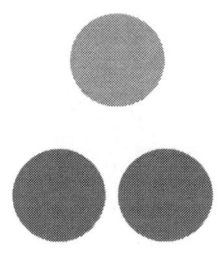

To do this, we need to select the blue circles and press Ctrl/Command+G. This will group the two circles. Now we can select all three circles and press the **align horizontally** button. This will treat the blue circles as the group they are and will center their group with the center of the orange circle. The result is this:

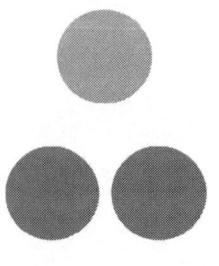

Distribution

Distribution refers to the equal distribution of objects on an axis. Here are four objects, placed with no consideration paid to the distance between them

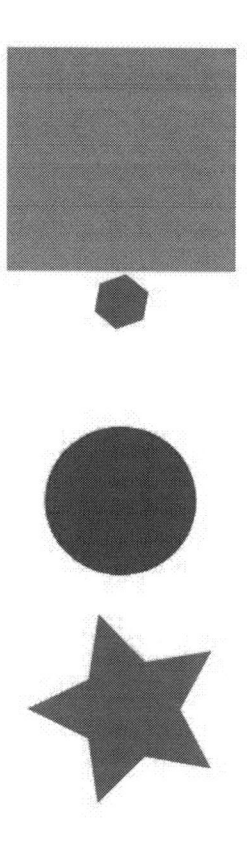

Selecting all of these objects and performing the **distribute vertically** operation will space them out in such a way as for the objects to be in equal distance from each other. Other vector graphics programs, such as Adobe Illustrator, allow you to select how the distribution will happen (eg. space the objects in such a way as the distance between them is equal **vs** spacing the objects so the distance between their *centers* is equal) but Gravit Designer does not allow that yet.

Here's the result of our distribution operation

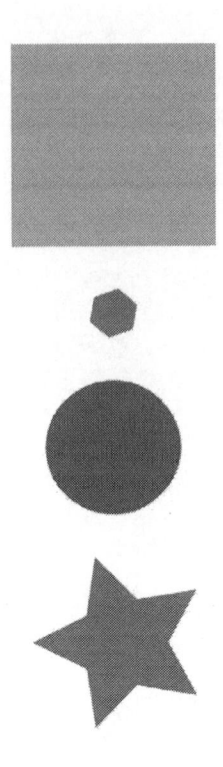

The distribution functions lie on the alignment panel, on the left of the alignment operation icons.

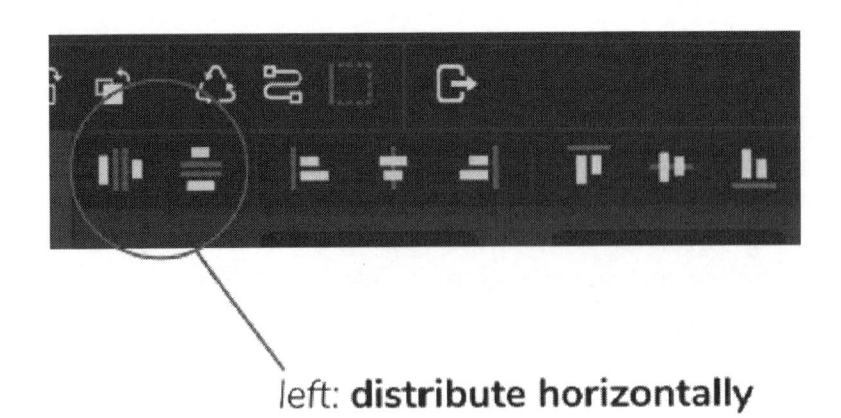

left: **distribute horizontally**
right: **distribute vertically**

Transformations: Chapter exercises

Exercise 1: Practice
This is an easy one: create lots of shapes and apply the Transform operations on them. Focus on scaling without messing up the ratio of objects and rotating objects using both the corner affordance and the rotation handle. Finally, use the arrow keys to move objects around the canvas and **Shift+arrow keys** to move them faster.

Exercise 2: Create a sword
Using everything you've learned so far, create a symmetrical sword with a handle, with its tip pointing upwards. Something similar, though not necessarily identical, to this:

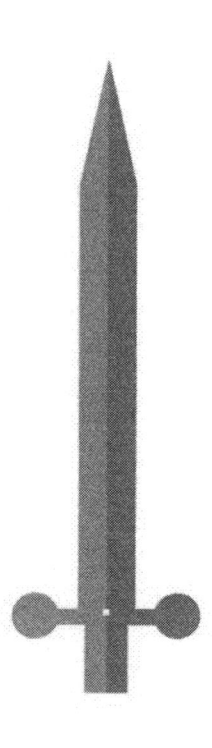

As always, if you're stuck let me know at sebastian212000@gmail.com

Chapter 8: Typography in Vector Graphics

Working with text and learning how to use typefaces, punctuation, kerning and other typographic concepts properly is outside the scope of this book. Instead, this chapter focuses solely on the artistic treatments you can apply to text in a vector graphics context. More specifically, the three basic treatments we'll be discussing are converting text to one or more paths, using text to mask content and placing text on a path.

First, let's place some text on the canvas.

The text tool

Every vector graphics program has a text tool and it almost always takes the form of a letter in the toolbar. Gravit Designer's text tool looks like this:

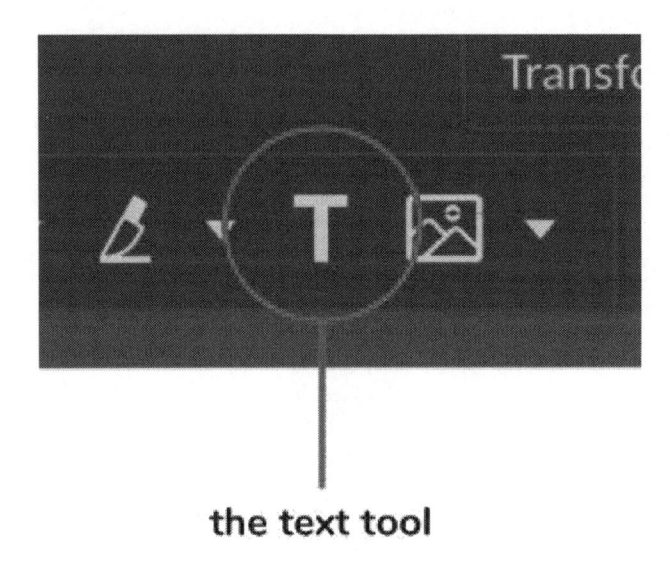

the text tool

When the text tool is clicked, your pointer changes into a tiny crosshair. Click that crosshair anywhere on the canvas and you're ready to start writing.

When the text tool is selected, the text appearance panel will open on the right side of the screen

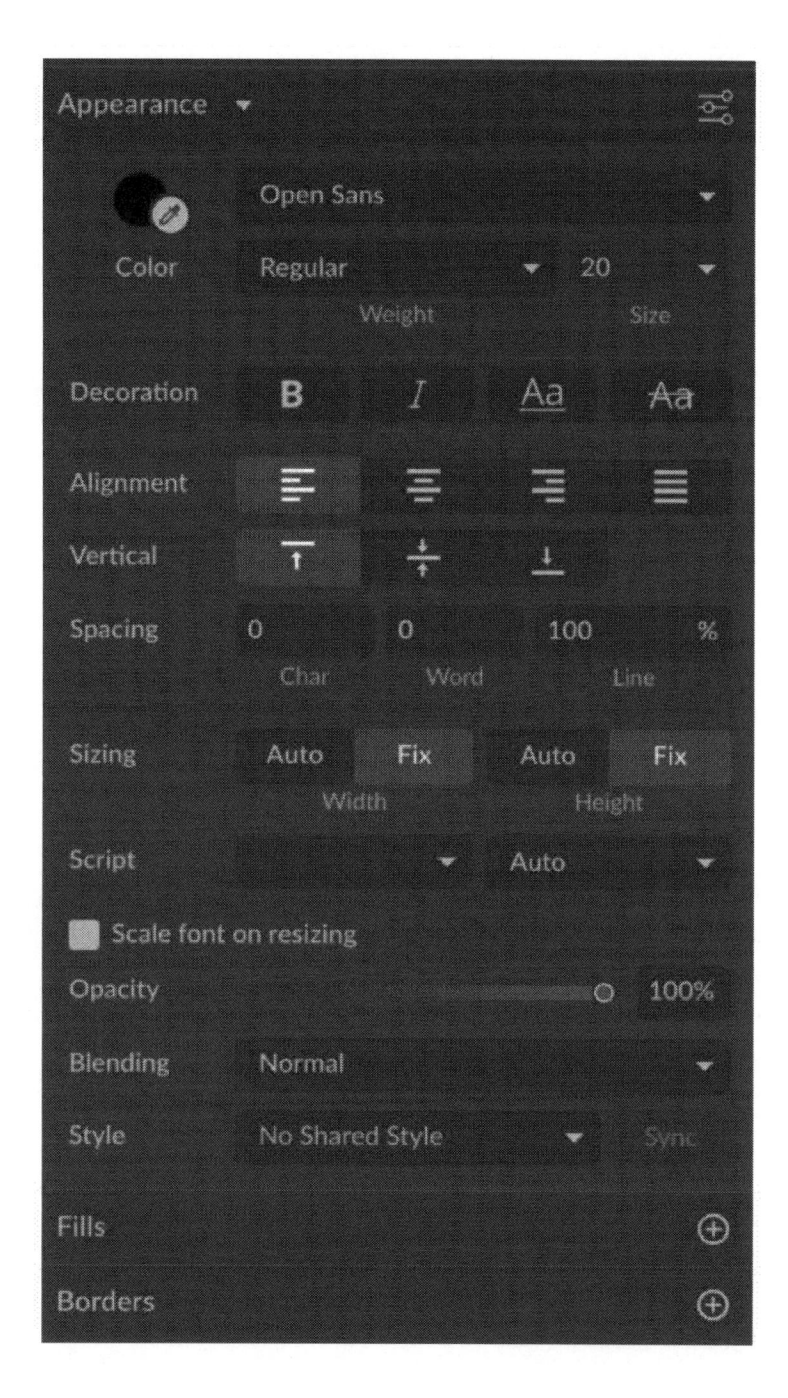

This panel allows you to select a **typeface** to use (it currently says 'Open Sans' in the text selection field; you can select from a huge variety of free fonts or import your own fonts by going to **File > Import > Add fonts**), the **size** of the text and the **weight** of the text (eg. light, regular, bold, etc).

The **decoration** section lets you apply attributes such as bold, italics, strikethrough and underlining to the text. Also pay attention to the **alignment** and **spacing** sections and, after writing some text on the canvas, experiment with them. Finally, enable the 'Scale font on resizing' option, which will resize the text whenever you scale its bounding box.

Entering **text appearance panel settings** by clicking on the   Sliders icon on the top right corner of the panel also lets you enable ligatures, apply subscript and superscript styles to text and change the capitalization scheme (all lowercase, all caps, first letter of each word to be capitalized, small caps).

For now, select the Text tool and write something on the canvas, preferably a short word like 'STATE' or 'WATER'. I'll go with 'THE FIFTH ELEMENT'. OK, not really. I'll go with 'LOVE', which is essentially the same thing. The typeface I chose to use (which should also be available to you by default in Gravit, if you want to use it) is called *Luckiest Guy*. If you're following along, you don't necessarily have to use this one, but you should still use a bold, heavy, impactful font to apply to your text. Here's my text

Converting text to path

There's an interesting duality in the objects we manipulate in vector graphics programs that we haven't discussed yet but which is extremely important and—seeing as we'll be using it extensively from now on—I should probably mention now.

Here's the thing: not every object you place on your canvas is the same. I know that sounds pretty obvious, but I'm not simply referring to a difference in shape or size or even color. What I'm talking about is the difference between a *path* and any other kind of object.

Think of it like this: when you draw a polygon on the canvas using the Shape tool, you don't simply get the option to change its stroke and fill. Drawing a polygon also gives you the ability to change its number of sides and the roundness of its corners. If you draw a circle, most vector graphics programs (including Gravit Designer) give you the option of removing a slice of a certain number of degrees from that circle. And if you write some text, the program gives you the ability to change the typeface you use to display your text.

All of the above are specialized attributes that you can only apply to certain objects. They are not universal attributes that you can apply everywhere—after all, what would changing the typeface of a circle look like?

However, there's an operation that takes all specialized shapes and, much like an overbearing professor at an English boarding school in a period drama, strips them of their uniqueness—a great equalizer, if you will. Different programs call this operation different things; in fact, some programs call this identical operation different things depending on what its converting.

Some names for this operation are

- Convert to curves
- Convert to outline
- Convert to path
- Create outlines
- Vectorize border
- Expand stroke

The names may vary wildly, but the final result is the same: a shape, letter, stroke and so on will be converted into a simple or compound path that you can manipulate more freely, stripped of all its specialness.

Since I struggled to understand what **expand stroke** does when I first came across it as a term, let me give you a short example. Take a look at this:

[black rectangle]

Here's my question: what are you looking at? Is it a really fat line or a really long rectangle? It can be any one of those things, right?

And indeed it can. The only way for you to know is to ask me and hope that I'll give you an honest answer. Since you asked nicely, I'm going to reveal that it's actually a really fat line, ie. a stroke with a very large width I created by using the Line primitive shape in Gravit Designer.
Here's what happens when I select it and perform the **expand stroke** (or, in Gravit Designer parlance, **vectorize border**) operation, by going to **Modify > Path > Vectorize Border**:

[black rectangle]

"What the hell, Antonis? That's the exact same thing, you dick!" I can hear you screaming.

But it is not. It merely looks the same. To really understand what is going on, let me go back and show you both of them with their bounding boxes.

First, the original line/stroke:

[black rectangle with thin white line and endpoints]

Now, the expanded stroke:

The original stroke does not even have a bounding box. It simply has a path running through it. The expanded stroke, on the other hand, is now a rectangle with a bounding box. In other words, *the expanded stroke is no longer a stroke; it's a rectangle with a black fill.*

The consequences of this conversion are significant: for one, you can no longer apply any stroke-specific attributes to the expanded stroke. There is no stroke width to speak of and you can no longer attach objects (like arrows) at either end of the stroke through the stroke settings panel. Since stroke-specific attributes are gone, you cannot use the dash and gap parameters, so you cannot make the stroke dashed by tweaking those parameters.

However, what you gain from this conversion is the ability to manipulate the (former) stroke as a shape in its own right. For example, if you select the newly-created rectangle, you can add a stroke to it to get something like this

In addition to this, you can use the direct selection tool to add **nodes/anchor points** to the shape to get results like this very easily

I still haven't mentioned the **direct selection tool** (or **subselect**, as Gravit Designer likes to call it), **anchor points** or the **pen tool** since they are more advanced concepts, but I'll be describing them briefly in their own chapter.

Back to text.

In the case of text, converting it into a path removes the ability for you to edit your text, change its typeface etc. but lets you perform some neat tricks that wouldn't be possible with your text in its special text state. I should mention that

Adobe Illustrator in particular has broken down this distinction in its latest versions, allowing you, by the use of its Touch Type tool, to do things to text that are simply not possible in other programs without converting your text into a plain path first.

However, since it's the principle of the thing we're discussing, we'll be converting our text into a path and using the result to do some cool stuff.

Neat trick 1: Applying a gradient fill to text

Fact: at the time of writing, Gravit Designer won't let you directly apply a gradient fill to text. If you select your text and go to the Fill section to select a fill type, the only type of fill you'll get is Color Fill, which kinda sucks.

Selecting our text and going to **Modify > Path > Convert to path** will turn the text object into a path, which means that your text is now non-editable (and also non-edible, but that's the way it always has been) but which also means that its Fill options have expanded considerably; they have essentially become the fill options that any other object would have. Go on, treat yourself by applying some gradient fills to your text. You deserve it.

Neat trick 2: Playing around with a single letter

Let's say that you've converted your text into a path, applied your gradient to it and now, at the height of your accomplishment, you've decided that your life has no meaning unless you move the letter 'O' in the word 'love' slightly higher than the rest of the letters. Besides the obvious (that you should seek professional help, and fast), I'm glad to report that there is indeed a way to do that.

Select the word that you've converted into a path and go to **Modify > Path > Split Path**. This will split your word into its component objects (in this case, the letters 'L', 'O', 'V' and 'E'). Gravit Designer is kinda buggy when it performs this operation, in that it fills any counters (the letters' enclosed empty spaces) with shapes that correspond to them, like below:

To remove the fills from the counters, select the counter-filling shapes and the entire letter (one letter at a time) and perform a subtraction operation on them. This will bring your counters back. Now that each of your letters is an independent path with restored counters (some letters, like 'N', don't have counters so there's nothing to restore), select one of the letters with your selection tool and drag it upwards:

Love

You can perform many other operations on these letters. For example, you can scale, rotate them etc.

Placing text on paths

Sometimes, you want your text to follow a path. You may be creating a badge, a logo or a cheesy birthday invitation. So how do you accomplish something like this?

I'M WRITING ON A CIRCLE, WHEEEEEE!

The answer is very simple: first, you create the path you want your text to follow. Then, you select the text tool from the toolbar and bring its crosshairs over the path you've made. Finally, you click and start writing. The text should now follow your path.

In the example I just showed you, I created two concentric circles. I gave the smaller one a fill and then used the bigger one as the path that my text would follow.

You're not limited to using primitive shapes as the paths that your text will follow. You can draw any arbitrary shape with your **pen tool** and then have the text follow that path, like so

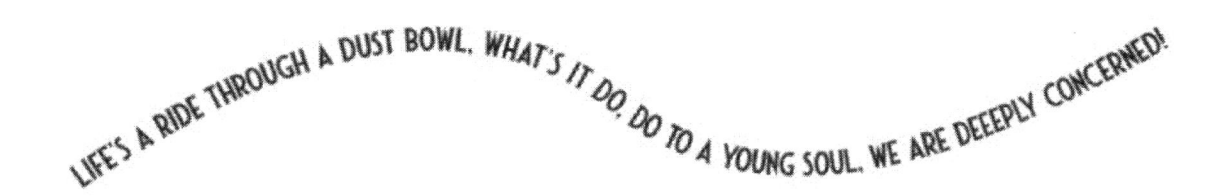

LIFE'S A RIDE THROUGH A DUST BOWL. WHAT'S IT DO, DO TO A YOUNG SOUL. WE ARE DEEEPLY CONCERNED!

Using text as a mask

Sometimes you'll see impressive compositions of bold, weighty text containing a photo that's evocative of the words being used. Stuff like this

Believe it or not, I made these in five minutes, including the time it took me to find the appropriate fonts & photos and a four-and-a-half minute visit to the toilet.

Creating images like these is dead simple, even for absolute beginners. To start with, you'll need some text, an appropriate typeface and an image. Obviously, this kind of thing works better if you use bold, impactful fonts that allow the photo to adequately show through, so select a font that fulfills those criteria. You can always download a photo to use from **unsplash.com**.

Start a new project and write something short and sweet on the canvas. Also, import your photo into your vector graphics program. In Gravit Designer you do this by going to **File > Import > Place Image**. Other programs have almost identical flows for importing an image. For example, Illustrator uses **File > Place**.

Now that you have both your text and your image in your project, it's time to apply your chosen typeface to the text. Click on the text tool and use it to highlight your text. Now change the default typeface to something you've selected.

Now that you have your text and your photo, it's time to place the photo into the text. There are at least two ways of accomplishing that:

- Select the photo and cut it (Ctrl-X). Then select the text and go to **Edit > Paste > Paste Inside Selection**. This will place the photo inside the text. Resize and move the photo to where you want it to be.
- Go to the Layers panel on the left of the screen. There, you should see two objects. One of them will be the text and the other will be the photo. Now click and hold on the photo object and drag & drop it on the text object. Success! The photo will now be a sublayer of the text object, showing though the text. Again, you can move and resize the photo freely, after it has been placed inside the text.

When you do any of these things, the text acts as a **clipping mask** to the photo. Think of a clipping mask as a window (or multiple windows) to underlying content. The mask allows some of the content to show through, while obstructing the rest of it.

Clipping masks are not simply a way to achieve the photo-inside-text effect; far from it. Clipping masks can also clip vector objects, making them perfect for adding detail and shading to illustrations, among other things. In the following chapter we'll take a look at clipping masks in more detail.

Working with text: Chapter exercises

Exercise 1: Practice

Open your vector graphics software and write some text using the text tool. Convert the text to path and play around with it. Using your selection tool, double click on the path and see what happens. The cursor should change appearance slightly. Use the new cursor to click on points along the path to create more anchor points. Move the anchor points by clicking on them and dragging them around. See how that changes the path.

In a new file, create a path and write some text along the path. Now convert the text itself into a path and apply a linear gradient to it.

Exercise 2: Using text as a mask

For this one, I want you to pour all your creativity into it. Think of a concept, situation or place that fascinates you or that you have a lot of affection for. Choose a word that relates to that concept and write it on your canvas using the text tool. Now do some research: find a font that fits the mood of your chosen concept and apply it to the text. Remember to use a font that's bold and impactful. Next, go to Unsplash (unsplash.com) and find a photo that's also relevant to the word you've chosen. Mask the photo with the text and send me the result at sebastian212000@gmail.com. I look forward to seeing what you'll come up with.

As always, if you're having any trouble with the exercises, don't hesitate to contact me at the aforementioned email address.

WANT TO LEARN MORE ABOUT TEXT & TYPOGRAPHY?

In case you're interested in learning more (much more!) about text, text manipulation, layout, fonts and typefaces, and supercharging yourself as a designer in general, consider picking up a copy of Clothes For Language: A typography handbook for designers, authors and type lovers, written by yours truly in the same easy-to-read, irreverent tone as this very book.

Chapter 9: Advanced Vector Techniques

Becoming proficient in vector graphics creation is more a matter of practice than a matter of reading a book. This is why, throughout this book, I've been asking you to follow along with my examples and do the exercises at the end of each chapter. If you've made it this far into the book without even opening your vector graphics software, now's probably the time to go back to the start of the book and do it properly.

If, on the other hand, you've been doing the exercises and putting what you've been learning into practice, you should now be able to create icons, logos, illustrations and text-based designs of a basic to intermediate level.

The skills I'll be discussing in this chapter fall outside the "5 core skills that you need to have" concept that formed the basis of this book. They are slightly more advanced skills that I've already mentioned in passing and, while their discussion will be brief, this chapter will be a nice primer for those of you who wish to dive deeper into the world of vector graphics. Let's get going!

Masking

We've already used masking to insert photos into text but there are many other use cases for masking. **Any shape can mask any other shape** by using one of the following three methods, two of which I've already mentioned in the Working with Text chapter:

1. Select the shape you want to mask and then cut (Ctrl/Cmd-X) it. Next, select the object you want to use as a mask and go to **Edit > Paste > Paste > Paste Inside Selection**. To paste the shape to-be-masked inside the masking shape, you can also use the shortcut **Alt+Shift+Ctrl+V** if you're a shape-shifting alien with three rectums and a thousand fingers. After the shape is placed inside the masking shape, you can move it around and use transform operations to your heart's content.
2. In the layers panel, drag and drop the object to be masked (A) onto the masking object (B). Now object A will be clipped by object B.
3. Bring the objects so that they partially overlap and select the Clip tool from the toolbar. Now the object in the back will clip the object in the front. The Clip tool looks like this:

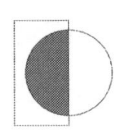

A very cool use case for clipping is adding details to an object that you don't want bleeding out to the rest of the artwork. Let's revisit the mountain scene I did in the chapter on Z-ordering and add a snowy peak to a plain ol' mountain. Let's get started by drawing a gray triangle (mountain) in front of a deep blue rectangle (sky). Now, using the Shape tool, draw some white triangles on the top corner of the triangle in a formation similar to this

I know that you're thinking "WTF is this?" right now but bear with me. Now select the white triangles only, use the Union boolean operation to unite them and then go to **Modify > Path > Convert to Path**. Finally, select the shape you just created and the big, gray triangle (the mountain) and click the Clip tool (or use one of the other methods I've described to accomplish the exact same thing). Here's the result:

Masking can also help you create papercraft-ish designs by applying an inner shadow effect (more on this in the Effects subsection) to the masking object:

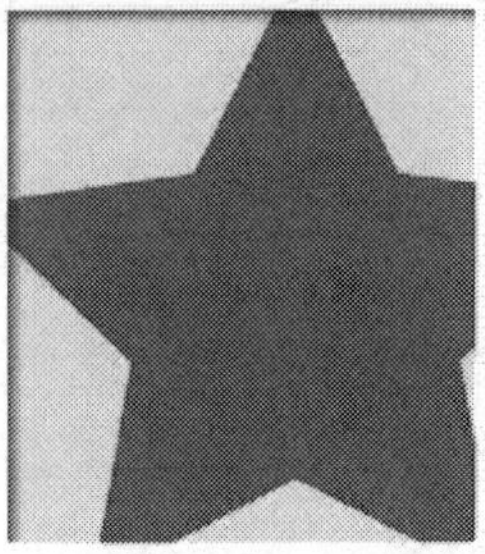

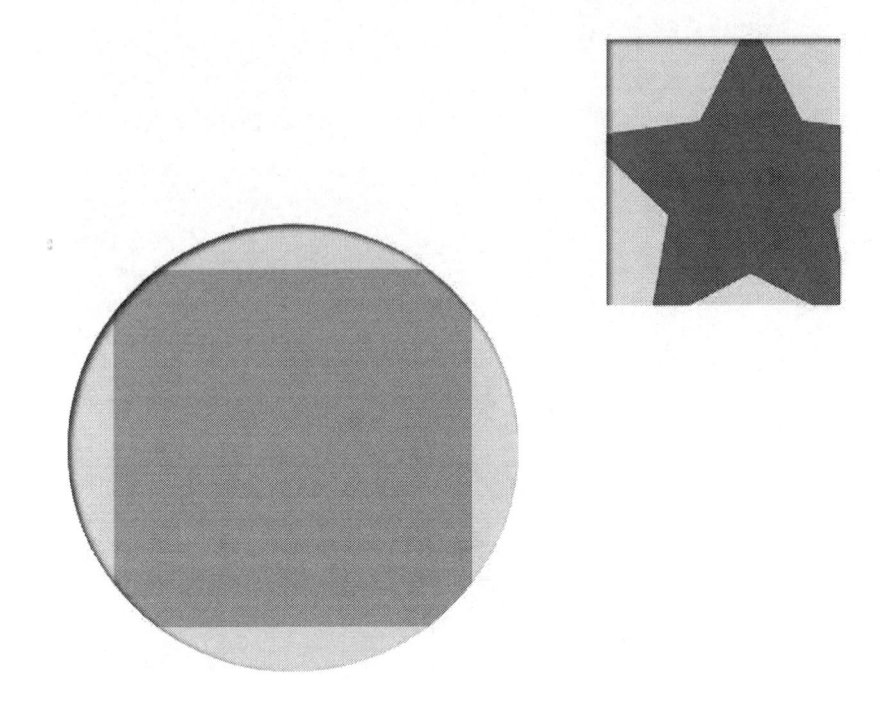

Effects

There is no shortage of effects for you to use in any vector graphics software. Adobe Illustrator offers two categories of effects: vector effects and Photoshop effects. Vector effects affect vector paths, with the result retaining its vector nature after processing (for example, the Zig-Zag effect takes a straight path and turns it into a zig-zagging line) while Photoshop effects are raster-based effects that don't change the underlying vector shape but instead generate pixels (for example, the Blur effect).

Affinity Designer and Gravit Designer offer no such distinction, which is unfortunate. At the time of writing, all of their effects are raster-based.

There's no point in going through all of the effects, since discovering them and using them creatively is part of the fun, but let's take a look at some of the most commonly-used ones. Follow along by creating a shape of your choosing on the canvas (I'll go with a circle).

The Effects panel is at the lower right part of the screen, as you can see here:

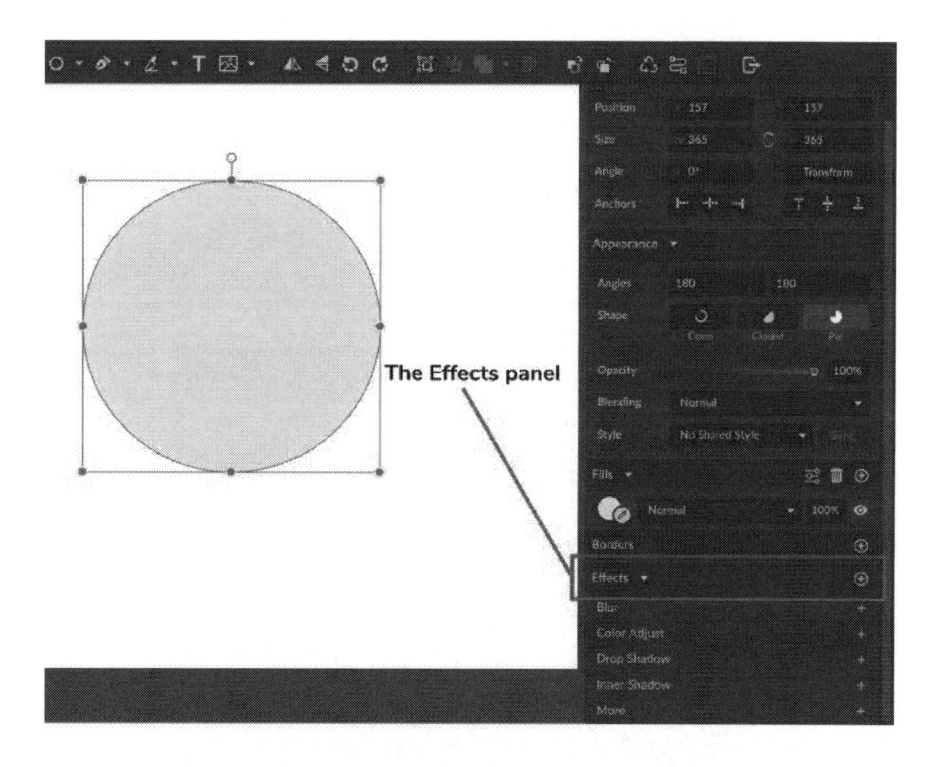

Here are some of the effects I use most often:

- **Blur**: it blurs stuff. I know, big surprise. Blur is amazing for adding glow to objects by following this recipe: **Create a dark background > Select the object you want to make glowy > Copy and paste the object in place so that you have to copies > Select the copy in the back (use the layers panel) and apply A LOT of blurring to it by increasing the radius.** Your object should now be glowing! This works so well that I've stopped using the Outer Glow effect altogether. Here's how the object looks before applying the procedure I've outlined

Here's how it looks with the procedure applied

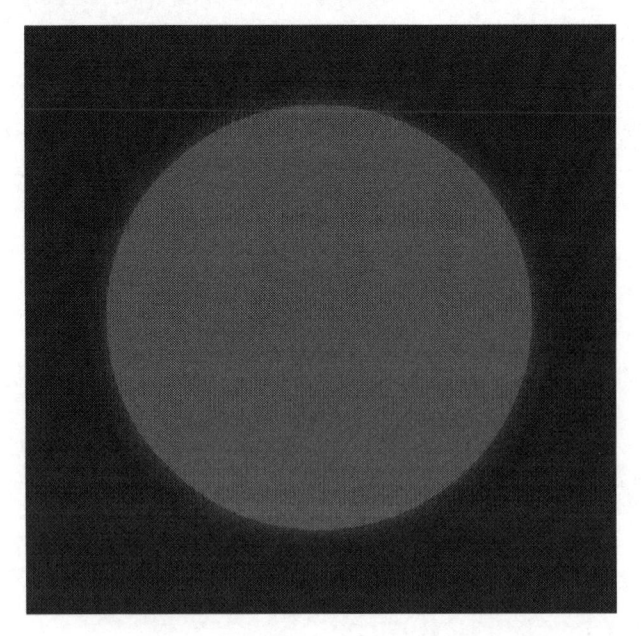

- **Drop Shadow & Inner Shadow**: This effect adds a shadow around or inside the object. It can definitely be overused so I avoid applying it, unless I'm going for a papercraft-like look.

- **Noise:** This effect adds some nice texture to objects, especially in combination with a gradient. Again, it can be overused, so apply it sparingly. Here's me applying this effect in combination with a gradient on our glowing orb from before:

Nice planet, huh?

There are many more effects for you to apply so go ahead and discover some of your future favorites. The fate of the world depends on it!

Pen tool, anchor points and bezier curves

Do you know what a bezier curve is? No? I don't blame you. Here's a few bodacious ones:

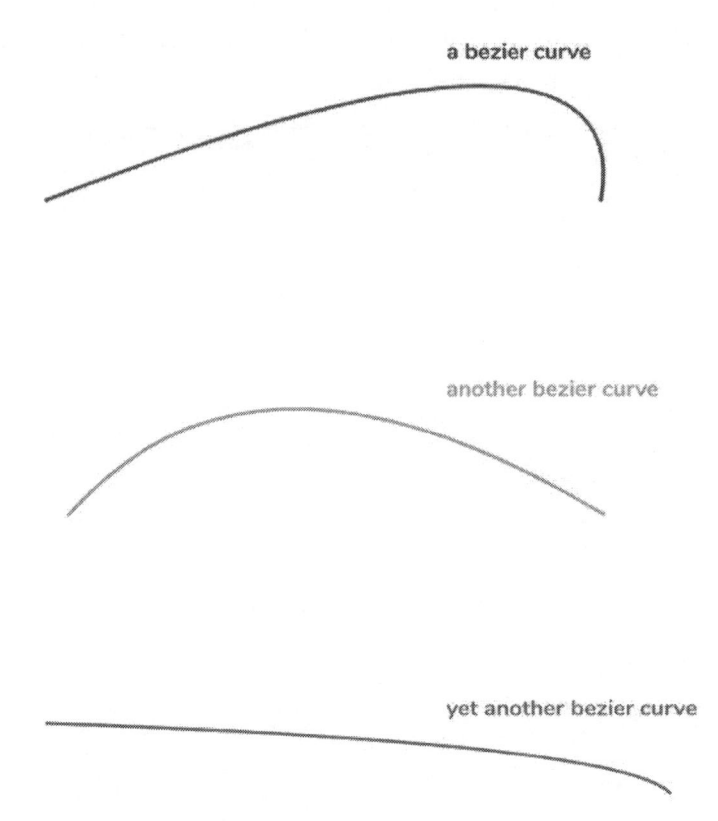

a bezier curve

another bezier curve

yet another bezier curve

After spending quite a while thinking that bezier curves look a lot like the chassises of cars when I first became familiar with them, I was vindicated when I read this on Wikipedia

> A Bézier curve is a parametric curve used in computer graphics and related fields. The curve, which is related to the Bernstein polynomial, is named after Pierre Bézier, **who used it in the 1960s for designing curves for the bodywork of Renault cars**.

Bezier curves are really important in the field of vector graphics, since they are what the **pen tool** generates when you draw with it.

The pen tool usually looks something like this

Even though its name may suggest that you can use it for freehand drawing, you cannot. To draw with the pen tool, you usually use your mouse to generate the curves and then manipulate their **anchor points** (also known as **nodes**) and the nodes' **handles** to create your object. If the object is even a little bit complex, it usually ends up being a chain of connected (or disconnected) bezier curves.

Here's an example of an object created using the pen tool, comprised of several bezier curves

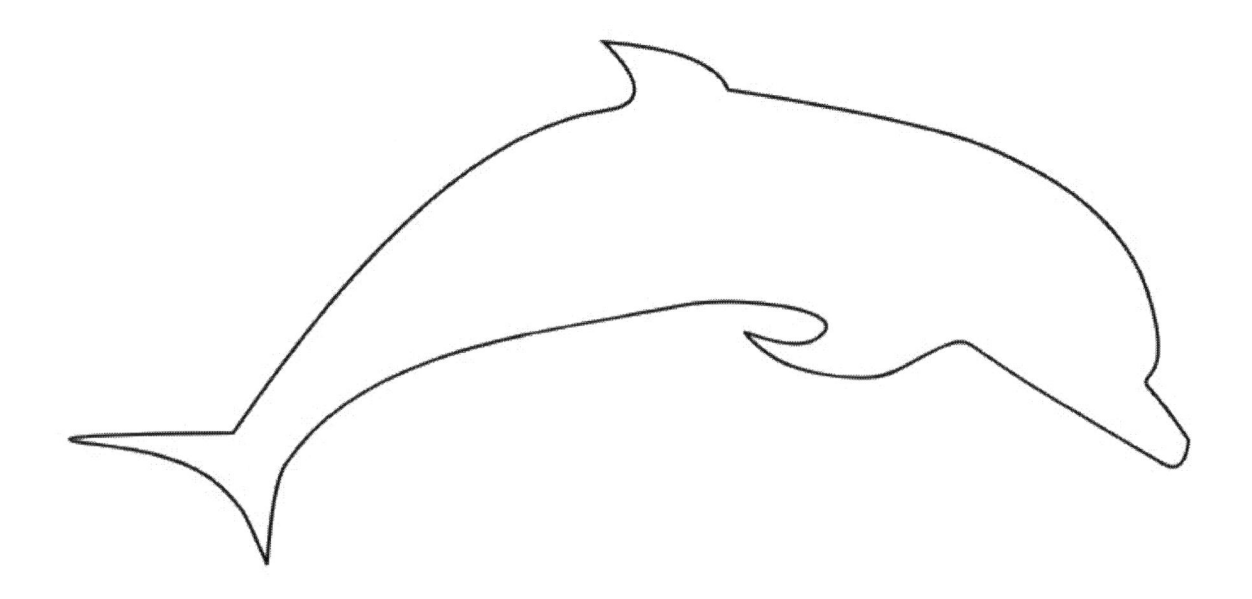

Want to see how it looks with the anchor points visible?

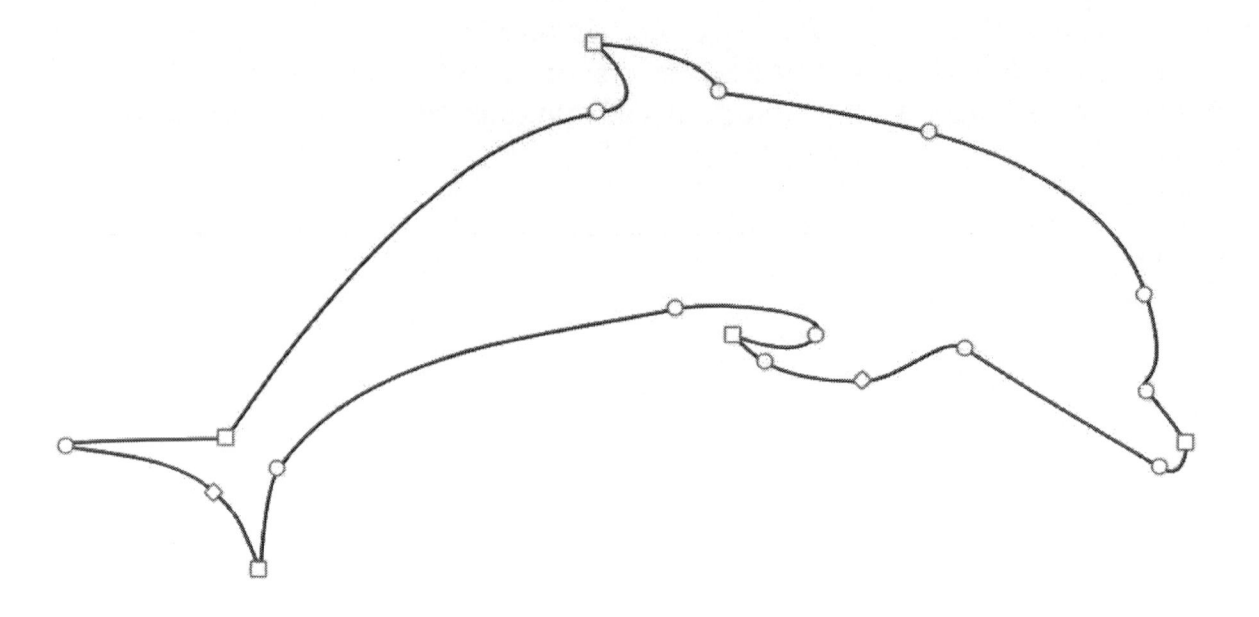

The curve between any two anchor points is a bezier curve. You may notice that some of them are not actual curves but straight lines.

Becoming familiar with the pen tool takes a little bit of practice, so load up your vector graphics software and let's take a look at it. I'll be using Gravit Designer as always but all vector software works rather similarly as far as the pen tool is concerned.

Straight lines & curves

Create a 768px by 768px canvas and select the pen tool. Click on the canvas once and release your mouse button. You'll notice that you now have a static (anchored) point where you clicked and a second point attached to your cursor that you can move around with your mouse. Select a second point on the canvas and click again.

Bam! You just draw a straight line with two anchor points.

Want to do something cooler? Start by doing the same thing as before: using the pen tool, click on a point on the canvas and release the mouse button. Now click somewhere else on the canvas but *before releasing the mouse button* move your mouse in any direction. You should see a bezier curve forming. When the curve is sexy enough for you, release the mouse button and there's your curve!

You'll notice that, if you try to click a third time on the canvas to add another section to your shape, the software will attempt to curve the new section towards the third point. If you don't want it to do that, but instead want the software **to create a sharp corner and a straight line towards the third point, you must hold down the Alt button and click on the last anchor point you laid down**. Definitely keep this in mind because it's something that'll definitely come up while you're creating a shape.

Now select the Subselect tool (or Direct Select, depending on the software you're using) and click on the bezier curve. The anchor points you've laid down should become visible, which will let you click on them with your direct select tool and manipulate them.

(Here's a nice tip: double clicking with the normal selection tool on a bezier curve will instantly turn your selection tool to the direct selection tool and give you access to the anchor points.)

But what does it mean to manipulate the anchor points? Moving them? Yes, but not only: you can also change their type.

Anchor point types

To demonstrate anchor point types, I'll ask you to do something first: using your pen tool, draw a straight line in the way I explained earlier: click once on the canvas to put down an anchor point and then click on another point on the canvas to create the straight line. The difference this time is that you shouldn't stop: click a third time on the canvas to continue drawing a second line at an angle to the first, something like this

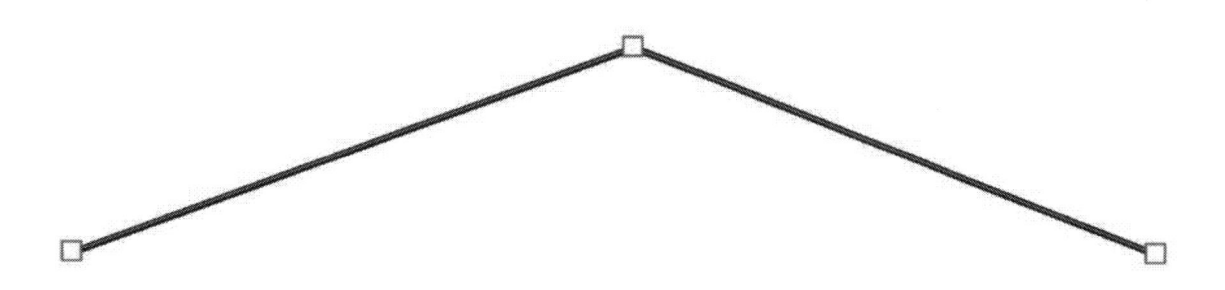

Using your direct selection tool, click on the middle anchor point. A panel will appear on the right, with a section allowing you to change the Joint (anchor) type:

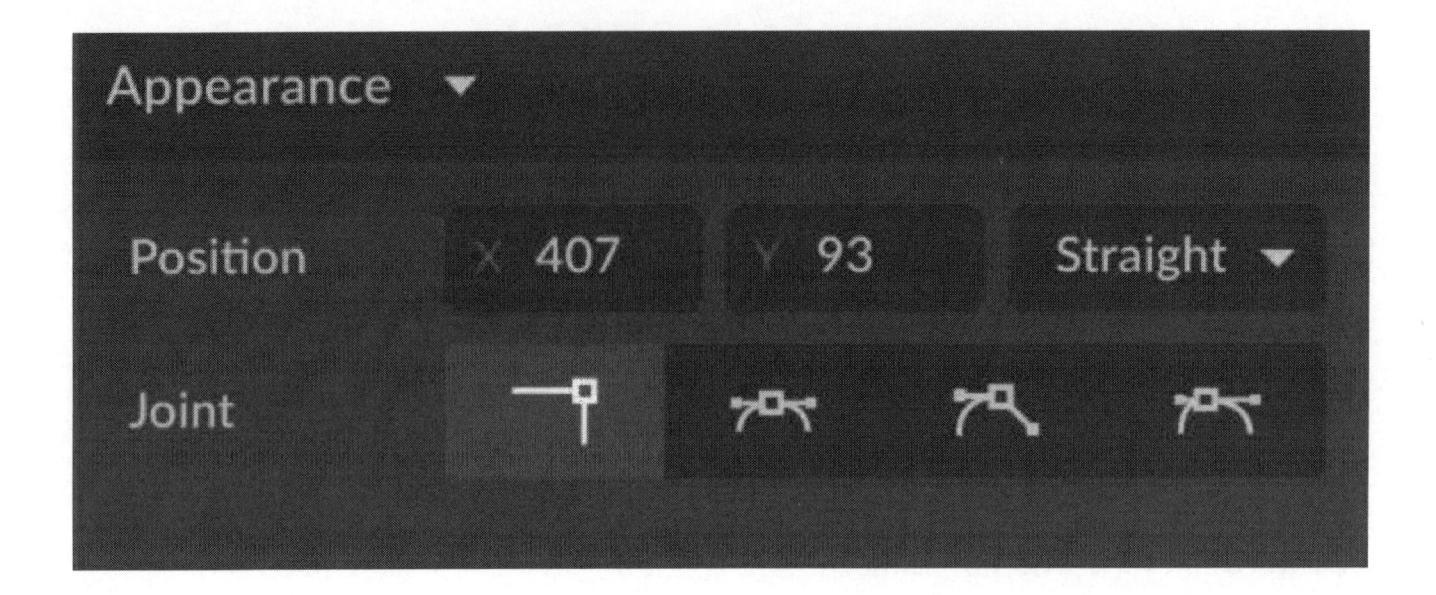

Currently, the joint type should be **Straight**. This denotes a sharp corner, which is the way it is right now. From either the dropdown menu on the panel or the icons in the Joint section, select **Mirrored**. This will turn the sharp corner into a curve:

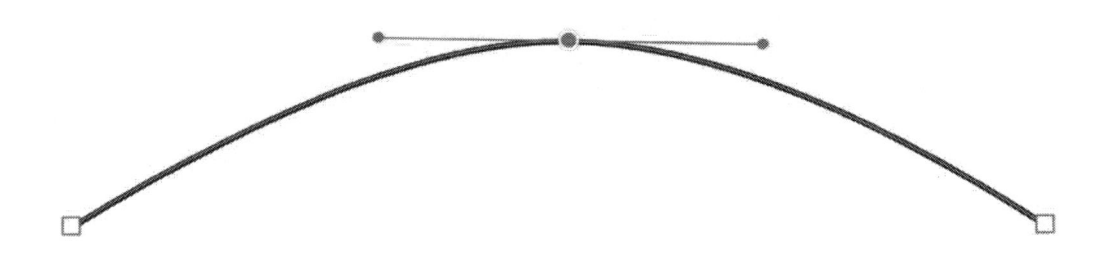

There are other anchor types to try (**Disconnected, Asymmetric, Connector**) that mainly refer to the behavior of the anchor **handles**, ie. the two lines that start from an anchor point when selected. Clicking and holding on the round ends of those handles lets you drag them, so that you can change their length and angle, thereby modifying the shape of the object itself. When using some anchor point types, the handles move in relation to each other, while with other anchor types they move independently of each other.

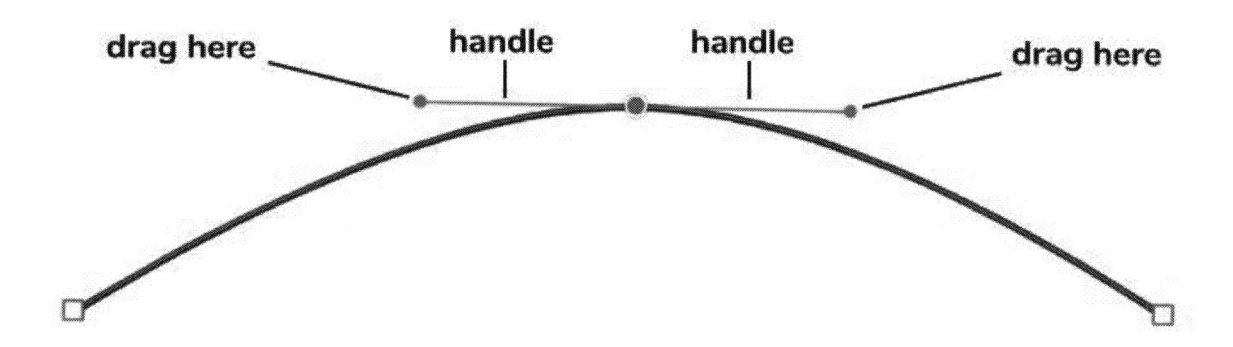

Your best bet, as with anything pen tool-related, is to open your software, create some objects with sharp corners and then experiment away. See what happens when you move the handles one way vs moving them another way, depending on the anchor type you've selected.

Finally, when you're using the direct select (subselect) tool, you can hover over the bezier curves themselves (not the anchor points) and change their shape by clicking on them, holding and dragging.

After you've played around with the pen tool for a bit, try to create actual objects that look like something recognizable. Learning how to use the pen tool effectively is a valuable skill, but it takes some practice.

Multi Selecting anchor points

Let's create a stylized wave using nothing but the pen and direct select tools. Create a new canvas and draw something like this:

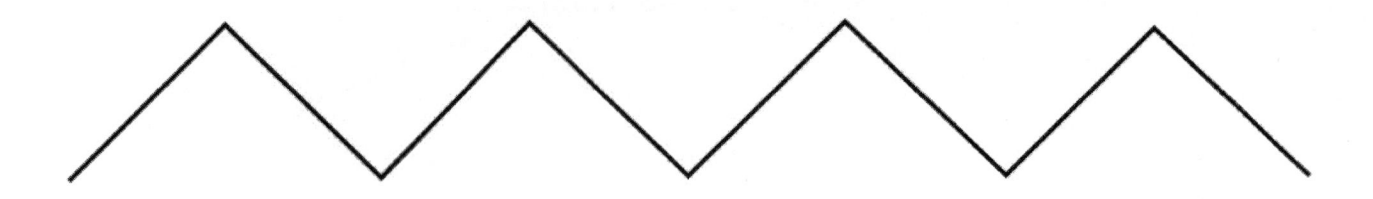

Creating this shape is very easy, as long as you remember two things

- **Enable snapping!** With snapping on (the magnet icon in your toolbar), you'll get guidelines letting you know whenever your anchor points are aligned on the Y-axis, so you can keep them there.
- **Hold Shift before you draw your lines**. This will ensure that the lines you're drawing will remain angled at multiples of 45 degrees.

Using your direct select tool, select all anchor points by holding down Shift and clicking on all of them individually (or including them all in a rectangular selection area created with the subselect tool). Now change the anchor type for all anchor points to **Mirrored:**

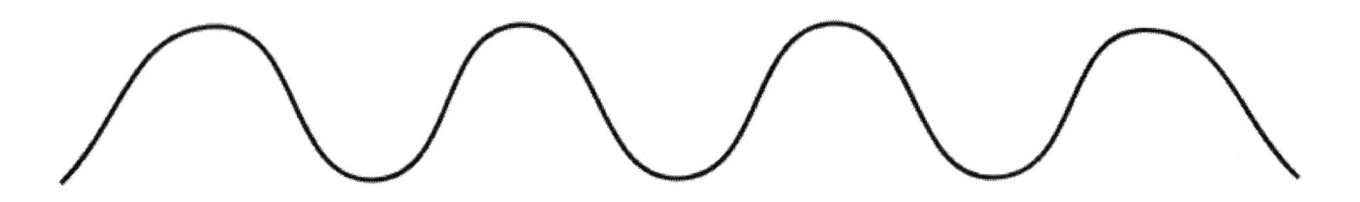

With all of the anchor points converted to mirrored, you get a nice wave-like graphic.

Adding anchor points to an existing shape / convert to path

You can add one on more anchor points to an existing path (and subsequently manipulate said points) by using the subselect tool or the pen tool. To do that, you simply click with the pen tool or the subselect tool on the point(s) on the path you want to add the anchor point(s) to. Removing an anchor point is as easy: click on the anchor point you want to remove and press 'Delete' on your keyboard.

Adobe Illustrator has specialized tools for adding (or removing) anchor points; when you click on the pen tool, you'll be able to access those tools.

Try to remember that certain vector graphics programs (with Gravit Designer being among them) won't let you add anchor points to specialized objects, such as rectangles, stars, polygons, etc. without converting them to a path first. So if you try to add an anchor point to a rectangle in Gravit and it's not working, first go to **Modify > Path > Convert to Path** and then try again.

Let's make a simple almost-envelope graphic to see how adding an anchor point works. First, either draw a rectangle yourself with the pen tool (remember that holding down Shift while you create your path will keep your line completely vertical or horizontal) or use the rectangle using the shape tool and then convert it to a path. Remove the fill and give it a good, thick stroke (that sounded vaguely sexual):

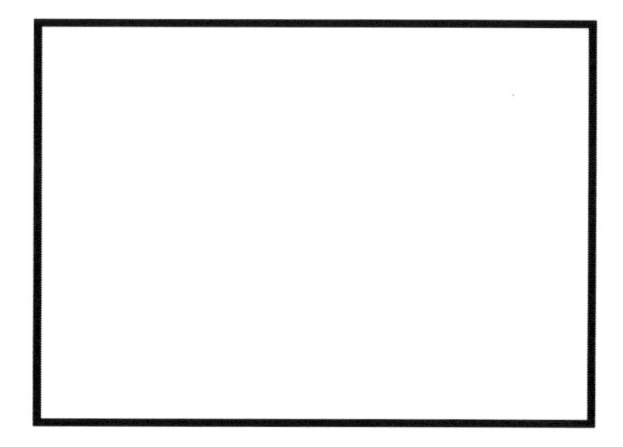

Perfect! Now, with the help of guidelines (you have snapping enabled, right?) add an anchor point in the middle of the top horizontal side using either the subselect or pen tool. If the guideline is not showing (sneaky motherfuckin' guideline), first add the anchor point, then select it with the subselect tool and then click on Align Center Horizontal in the alignment panel to place it perfectly in the center of the side. Now hold Shift down to make the anchor point move completely vertically and drag & drop it lower (near the center of the rectangle should be good):

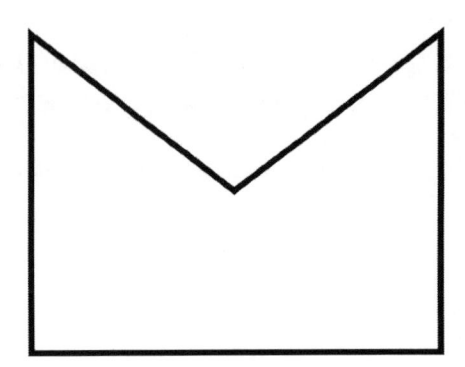

If you're a stickler for detail (please be), add a line to the top of the shape with the same thickness as the rest of it to finish the graphic

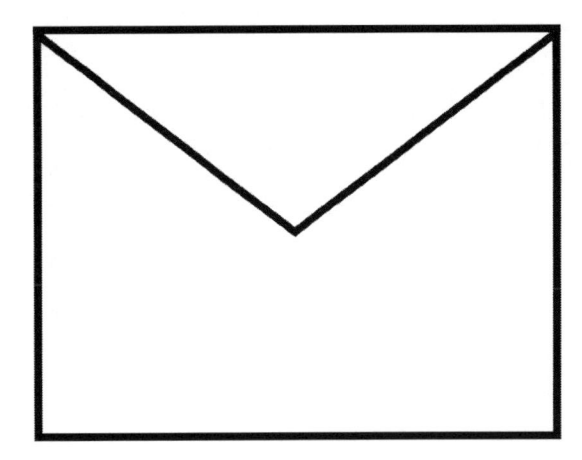

As an exercise, try to think of a couple of alternative ways you could have achieved the same result and then go ahead and do it.

Closed paths vs Open paths

There's not much to be said about open paths vs closed paths, other than to explain what they are, since it's a term you're bound to come across.

Here's an open path

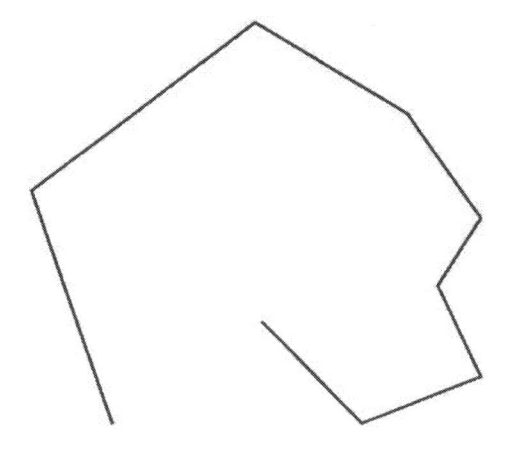

And here's a very similar closed path

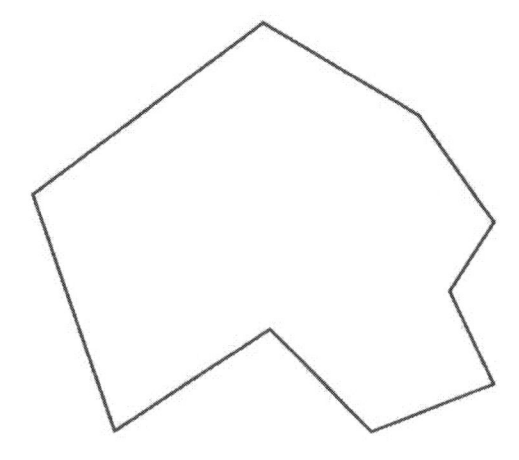

The difference should be obvious: the open path has a beginning and an end. It's clearly a line segment and not a polygon. In other words, it has **endpoints**.

The closed path, on the other hand, does not have a beginning or an end. It has no endpoints; it's simply an irregular polygon.

You can select to leave a path open or simply click back to the starting anchor point to close it. Unlike what you might think, an open path can have a fill. It doesn't simply spill out on the rest of the canvas, unlike what happens in MS Paint:

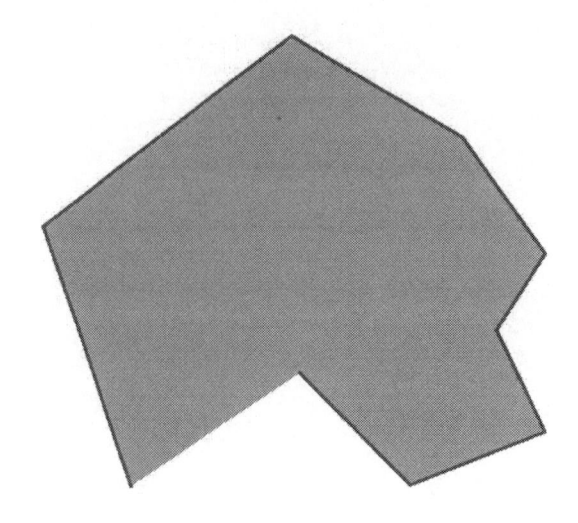

Practicing with the pen tool

I want to finish this chapter by encouraging you to practice with the pen tool, as it is something you'll be using regularly if you decide to pursue a career in a field relating to vector graphics (graphic design, illustration, etc).

The best way to do it is to draw a simple line sketch with a pencil or a pen on a piece of paper, take a photo, import it into your vector graphics software (**File > Import > Place Image** or **File > Place…**) and try to trace the sketch with the pen tool. You'll mess up a little at first but keep trying. It shouldn't take long for you to become relatively proficient at using it.

CONCLUSION

As we draw the curtains on this exploratory guide into the world of vector graphics, it's important to take a moment to reflect on the journey we've embarked upon together. From the foundational blocks to the complex nuances of boolean operations, each page turned has brought new insights and broadened our digital horizons.

Beginning with an introduction to vector graphics, we established the fundamental difference between vectors and rasters—clarity at any size, a concept that echoes the boundless potential of your new skill set. You've been equipped not only with the technical knowledge of file formats and conversions but also with a deeper understanding of when and why to choose vector graphics over their pixel-based counterparts.

In navigating the basic tools, you've grasped the importance of precision and flexibility. You've learned how to select, manipulate, and transform shapes, taking control of the digital canvas with a confident hand. The exercises in Chapter 4 solidified your command over primitive shapes, as you learned that complexity is built from simplicity, a truth that resonates in both design and life.

Through the layered lessons of z-ordering, your designs gained depth and your perspectives, a new dimension. With boolean operations, you dissected and reconstructed shapes, learning that design, much like problem-solving, often requires deconstruction before synthesis.

The transformative magic of scaling, rotating, and translating shapes introduced you to the ballet of vector design, a choreography of elements that harmonizes to produce visual symphonies. Text, the spoken word of design, became another instrument in your repertoire as you mastered its flow and form on the vector stage.

Advancing to masking and effects, you've added complexity to your compositions, exploring the subtleties of visual storytelling. With each bezier curve and anchor point, your digital pen danced, and your creations began to reflect a personal signature, a style uniquely yours.

Now, as we reach the end of this guide, it's essential to recognize that this conclusion is merely a pause, not an end. The world of vector graphics is dynamic and constantly evolving. New software updates, design trends, and creative challenges await you. The conclusion of this book is the commencement of your real-world application of vector graphics—a world where your newfound skills will continue to grow, evolve, and adapt.

You are no longer beginners in the realm of vectors but emerging artists and designers poised to leave your mark on the digital canvas. The exercises you've completed are stepping stones to projects that will challenge and excite you. The knowledge you've acquired is a launchpad for innovation and creation.

As you close this guide, take pride in the progress you've made and look forward with anticipation to the myriad possibilities that lie ahead. Vector graphics is not just a tool; it's a language of visual expression that you now speak. Use it to tell your stories, to bring your visions to life, and to connect with the world in ways only you can.

Celebrate the completion of this guide as a milestone in your lifelong learning journey. May the vectors you create be as boundless as your imagination, as precise as your dedication, and as impactful as your potential.

As we journey beyond the final chapters of this guide, it's imperative to recognize the transformative power of the knowledge you now hold. Each chapter was not just a lesson in vector graphics, but also a stepping stone towards a deeper comprehension of digital art and design. Like a map that has been charted, the skills you've acquired are coordinates to destinations yet unknown, filled with the promise of creative exploration and discovery.

The Vector Graphics 2024 Guide for Beginners has been more than just a collection of tutorials; it has been a narrative of growth and an affirmation that with the right tools and a persistent spirit, complexity can be unraveled into understandable elements. It's a testament to the truth that great designs emerge from understanding the interplay between shape, color, and form.

Your initiation into the world of vector graphics began with an understanding of its core — a world where lines are not just strokes but paths that define the boundaries of imagination. You've seen firsthand how a simple shift in a bezier curve can alter the mood of an illustration, how the interplay between text and image can narrate a story without a single spoken word.

As you forged ahead into the realm of practical application, you grappled with z-ordering, layering objects to create depth and focus. This essential aspect of vector graphics is akin to setting the stage for a play. Each element is an actor, each layer a different plane of the story being told. You've learned to direct this cast with a precise vision, ensuring that every part contributes to a cohesive whole.

Boolean operations emerged not just as a tool but as a philosophy, where the combination and subtraction of shapes are reminiscent of the way we build ideas—layer upon layer, concept upon concept. You've embraced the iterative process of design, recognizing that the first draft is seldom the last, and that the act of creation is one of continuous refinement.

Transformations taught you that objects in your designs are not static. They can move, grow, and change orientation, allowing for dynamic compositions that breathe life into static images. You learned that the control points are the strings by which you can conduct the elements of your design, much like a puppeteer brings a marionette to life.

The chapter on text opened your eyes to the power of typography. You now understand that type is not merely a vessel for content but an essential design element that can reinforce the message and emotion of your work. The exercises in kerning, leading, and tracking have imbued you with an appreciation for the nuance of type, a subtle art that speaks volumes.

As you ventured into more advanced techniques, you discovered the artistry within the technical. Masking and effects are not just about altering perceptions but about expanding the narrative of your designs. You've learned to peel back layers, to reveal and conceal aspects of your work, crafting a visual interplay between what is seen and what is suggested.

Pen tools, anchor points, and bezier curves are the vocabulary of vector graphics, and you've become fluent in this language. You learned to trace the outlines of your visions with precision, to control the tension of curves, and to anchor your points in space, translating concepts into tangible designs.

The journey you embarked upon has been rich with challenges, exercises, and real-world applications, and the conclusion of this book is not an end to learning but an invitation to continue expanding your horizons. The field of vector graphics does not stand still; it is continually propelled forward by innovation and creativity. You are now part of that evolutionary process.

Armed with the knowledge and skills from this guide, you are poised to join a community of creators who share your passion for clean lines, vibrant colors, and scalable art. Your work will no longer be confined to the pages of a tutorial but will extend into the spaces of the internet, print media, branding, and wherever your creative endeavors may lead.

As you continue to craft your vector masterpieces, remember that every point you plot, every path you draw, and every node you adjust contributes to your growth as a designer. In this digital age, where visual content reigns supreme, your ability to create with vectors is not just a skill—it's a superpower.

In closing, let this guide be a launching pad for your imagination and the start of an exciting, creative adventure. Your exploration of vector graphics does not conclude with the last page of this book but continues in every project you undertake, every design you create, and every boundary you push in this vast, dynamic landscape of digital art.

Let the journey continue, and may your vectors always point towards new horizons.

Printed in Great Britain
by Amazon